Free To Say No?

Free To Say No?

Free Will and Augustine's Evolving Doctrines
of Grace and Election

Eric L. Jenkins

WIPF & STOCK · Eugene, Oregon

FREE TO SAY NO?
Free Will and Augustine's Evolving Doctrines of Grace and Election

Copyright © 2012 Eric L. Jenkins. All rights reserved. Except for brief quotations in critical publications or reviews, no part of this book may be reproduced in any manner without prior written permission from the publisher. Write: Permissions, Wipf and Stock Publishers, 199 W. 8th Ave., Suite 3, Eugene, OR 97401.

Wipf & Stock
An imprint of Wipf and Stock Publishers
199 W. 8th Ave., Suite 3
Eugene, OR 97401

www.wipfandstock.com

ISBN: 13: 978-1-62032-225-3

Manufactured in the U.S.A.

Contents

Acknowledgments / vii
Introduction / ix

1 **DEFENDING FREE WILL IN THE EARLY WORKS** / 1
   Before *Free Will*
   Free Will
   After *Free Will*

2 **DEFINING FREE WILL IN THE MIDDLE WORKS** / 32
   Before *To Simplician*
   To Simplician
   Confessions to *Punishment and Forgiveness of Sins*
   Spirit and the Letter

3 **DENYING FREE WILL IN THE LATER WORKS** / 62
   Nature and Grace
   Perfection of Human Righteousness and *Deeds of Pelagius*
   Grace of Christ and *Original Sin*
   Letter 194 and *Answer to the Two Letters of the Pelagians*
   Answer to Julian, Enchiridion, and *City of God*
   Grace and Free Choice, Letter 217, and *Rebuke and Grace*
   Predestination of the Saints and *The Gift of Perseverance*
   Unfinished Work in Answer to Julian

4 **EVALUATION OF THE DOCTRINES OF GRACE, ELECTION, AND THE WILL** / 101
   Identifying the Changes in Augustine's View of the Will
   Affirming God's Just, Merciful, and Loving Nature
   Final Thoughts

Bibliography / 121

Acknowledgments

I WOULD LIKE TO express my deepest love and appreciation to my wife, Jacquelin, whose love and patience allowed me to focus so much time and energy on the completion of this book. Her listening ear and insightful comments and questions helped me to clarify my thoughts and develop my conclusions in a more coherent manner. This project would not have been possible without her support.

I would also like to acknowledge the loving patience of my three precious children: Joshua, Sheila Joy, and Jeremie. They were forced to listen to far too many dinner time discussions of Augustine, grace, free will, and other topics, yet they never complained and frequently asked thoughtful questions. Showing them all the love and attention they deserved, while delving into the voluminous writings of Augustine and his interpreters, was a task I may not have done as well as I would have liked, but their love and support always remained consistent.

Finally I would like to acknowledge the assistance of Tony Lane, professor at London School of Theology. The conclusions of this book are not his, but his gentle interrogations helped me fill in my logic flaws, strengthen my arguments, and limit my polemical tendencies.

Introduction

AN ENORMOUS EARTHQUAKE ROCKED North Africa at the end of the fourth century and its repercussions continue to be felt throughout the world today. The epicenter of the quake was an unlikely place, the quiet study of a newly appointed priest named Aurelius Augustine, in the city of Hippo. The first rumbles began around 396, as Augustine wrestled with the biblical teachings of grace, election, and the freedom of the will. His conclusions sent tremors through monasteries from North Africa to France and influenced the development of religious, philosophical, psychological, and even political thought for the next 1600 years. Henry Chadwick, noted historian of the early church, credits him with influencing Anselm, Aquinas, Calvin, Luther, Pascal, Kierkegaard, and Nietzsche. He claims Augustine's psychological analysis even "anticipated parts of Freud."[1] Many scholars believe Augustine shaped Western theology like no other person in church history, since the apostle Paul. His ideas were important in the foundation of the Catholic Church, but they also inspired the great Reformers. Many of the issues that are still being hotly debated in the church today find their roots in the varying interpretations of the teaching of Augustine.

None of those issues have stirred up more debate over the centuries than his doctrines of grace, election, and free will. Was man's destiny preordained by God's elective decrees before the foundation of the world, or is he the "captain of his own ship"? Does God love all of his creation or only the elect? Do we have limited autonomy or are we so dependent on him that we cannot do anything good unless his grace causes us to do it? Are we puppets, with God pulling our strings, or is it possible that even God himself doesn't know for sure what is going to happen next? These are just a few of the questions that emerge from a study of Augustine's writings.

---

1. Chadwick, *Augustine: Short Introduction*, 4.

Introduction

Despite his enormous influence on Western Christianity, most Christians, including most pastors and church leaders, know very little about what he wrote. One reason for this deficit is the vast amount of writing attributed to Augustine. He was a prolific author and the sheer volume of his writings has been compared to a theological Swiss Alps. Since it would take many books to study all the topics he covered, this book will focus on his doctrines of grace and election, with particular interest in their relationship to his theory of free will. Most scholars readily agree that Augustine's doctrines of election and grace went through major changes as he wrote. Augustine himself confessed to frequent vacillations in his views, saying, "I admit that I try to be of the number of those who write by advancing in knowledge, and advance by writing."[2] There is, however, a great deal of disagreement over how these changes affected his theory of free will.

There are at least three different approaches to evaluating Augustine's theories of free will. The first approach seeks continuity by interpreting his later predestinarian teaching in light of his early teachings on the freedom of the will. Eugene Portalié and Etienne Gilson are two scholars who advocate this approach. Portalié denies accusations that Augustine, «sacrificed freedom of the will on the altar of divine determinism.»[3] He insists, "Augustine never retracted his principal ideas on freedom of choice; he never modified his thought on the factor which is its essential condition, that is, the complete power of choosing or determining itself."[4] Gilson agrees, "we have never been able to find the least change, philosophically speaking, in any of his major ideas."[5] He believes that all of Augustine's works present grace as "irresistible without being constraining."[6] This approach argues that Augustine's early concept of free will remained consistent to the very end.

The second approach seeks continuity by attempting to harmonize Augustine's early and later works with each other. Carol Harrison suggests Augustine's early view of the will, "never shared the classical ideal of human autonomy and self determination," that some scholars have attributed

2. Augustine, *Letter 143*, 150.
3. Portalié, *Guide*, 197.
4. Ibid.
5. Gilson, *Christian Philosophy*, 310–11.
6. Ibid., 155.

to it. She denies there was a dramatic break in his later theology.⁷ Eugene TeSelle hopes to avoid inconsistencies between the early and later works by suggesting that God's gifts of faith and love never involved immediate divine action on the will. Grace in the later works merely produced an inclination to believe that could be consented to or dissented from.⁸ John Burnaby says Augustine always resisted the idea of the compelled will and claims the final theological system which goes by his name, "is in great part a cruel travesty of Augustine's deepest and most vital thought."⁹ Burnaby and TeSelle both admire the majority of his writings, yet wish that he had included stronger language about the possibility of refusing grace. They admit, however, the texts may not support such a possibility.¹⁰

This brings us to the third approach, where scholars like James Wetzel, John Rist, William Babcock, and J. Patout Burns suggest Augustine's later doctrines of grace and election call into question his early theory of free will. Wetzel argues that TeSelle and Burnaby's attempt to amend Augustine's view of grace to make grace resistible is, "endeavoring to do surgery with a meat ax. Little of Augustine's thought after 396 would survive the operation."¹¹ He sees incongruity between Augustine's early commitment to "voluntary willing" and his later allowance for "involuntary sin." He alleges that Augustine's later view "departs significantly" from his early view.¹² Rist sees the impossibility of refusing grace, found in Augustine's later works, as something which poisons his entire position.¹³ Babcock suggests the notion that sin must be a voluntary act of the will, began to slip from Augustine's grasp after his debate with Fortunatus.¹⁴ Burns finds changes after *To Simplician* do not express a harmonious development of previously stated principles, but rather, a replacement of early principles "by their contraries."¹⁵

The varied approaches of these Augustinian scholars reveal to us the nature of the debate we are entering. This book proposes that the

---

7. Harrison, *Rethinking*, 19.
8. TeSelle, *Augustine the Theologian*, 330–1.
9. Burnaby, *Amor Dei*, 231.
10. Wetzel, *Augustine and the Limits of Virtue*, 200.
11. Ibid., 202.
12. Ibid., 97.
13. Ibid., 201.
14. Babcock, "Augustine on Sin and Moral Agency," 35.
15. Burns, *Development*, 8.

Introduction

key issue in this debate is whether or not the human will has freedom to dissent from either the influence of carnal lust or the drawing of God's grace. Augustine's early writings appear to affirm the will's ability to either assent to or dissent from the perceptions, desires and influences which present themselves to it.[16] His later writings, on the other hand, tend to present God as the one who predetermines human wills. This move to the eternal predestinating decree, argues Creswell, "effectively destroyed human free choice of the will . . . and results in a redefinition of freedom and freedom of the human will."[17] We will evaluate whether this judgment is warranted. Eleonore Stump speculates that Augustine could have maintained both his early and late views without any contradiction if he had continued to claim that the will was able to reject the grace of God, but she admits Augustine's view of predestination might not have allowed him to accept this adjustment.[18] This will be the most important issue we will explore in this book. Does Augustine allow the will power to say, "No" to the drawing influence of grace? If he does not, then in what sense does he affirm freedom of the will?

The young Augustine clearly defended freedom of the will against Manichean determinism, but his opponents, who believe his latter theories of grace and election compromised his teachings on the free will, accuse him of renouncing freedom of the will in his later works. Augustine continued to defend free will in his later works, *Retractations*[19] and the *Gift of Perseverance*,[20] Yet, on another occasion claimed he had "labored in defense of the free choice of the human will; but the grace of God conquered."[21]

We will study Augustine's works chronologically in order to understand how developments in his doctrines of grace and election influenced his understanding of the free will, especially its power to say "No." This study will include a liberal number of quotes from Augustine's works, so that he is allowed to speak for himself. We will, of course, attempt to exegete the meaning of his words to grasp what he is teaching. We will

---

16. Creswell, *St. Augustine's Dilemma*, 69.
17. Ibid., 105–6.
18. Stump, "Augustine on Free Will," 141–2.
19. Augustine, *Retractations*, 1.8.3.
20. Augustine, *Gift of Perseverance*, 20.52–53.
21. Augustine, *Retractations*, 2.27.

explore the modifications he made along the way, paying particular attention to crucial moments of major change. Finally, we will make some judgments as to whether these varied positions can be reconciled into a consistent theological system or whether they devolve into contradictory theories marked by inconsistency.

Chapter 1

Augustine's Early Works

Before *Free Will*

We will divide Augustine's writings into three categories: the early works, the middle works, and the later works. These divisions represent significant shifts in his theology. The early writings reflect his optimistic view of human nature and his belief in conditional election—the belief that God chose who to save based on his foreknowledge of human faith. His initial understanding of the interaction between free choice and grace is based on the principle that humans can either assent to God's gracious offer of salvation or refuse his gift.[1] The middle writings send theological rumblings through Western Christianity, when Augustine rejects foreknown faith as the basis for election and proposes a doctrine of divine predestination.[2] Yet, he also says the will is called congruently, so that it remains free to either assent to or dissent from grace's call. The later writings set off more shockwaves, as Augustine adopts a darker understanding of man's bondage to sin to deal with the rising tide of Pelagianism. He comes to believe, "No one can delight in the law of God except when God directly arouse the affections."[3] This leads him to posit grace as the cause of the will's assent and to deny the theory of free will he had proposed in his early works. We will look carefully at important works from each of these three periods to discern how Augustine modified his views both within each period and between the periods.

1. TeSelle, "Engaging Scripture," 26.
2. Ibid.
3. Ibid.

The early works reflect his theological battles against the Manichees, a deterministic Gnostic group. These works have fewer scriptural references than his later works, though they are deeply theological. His desire to know God had inspired his involvement with the Manichees, the skeptics, and the Neo-Platonists. He was already asking important questions about God, evil, and the nature of the soul in these works. Neo-Platonism, which helped him to break with the Manichees, led him to envision Christianity as the fulfillment of Platonism. He was convinced that if the great Platonists had been alive in his day, they would certainly have become Christians. His optimistic opinion of the harmony between Christianity and Platonism eventually faded, but the influence of Neo-Platonic writers like Porphyry and Plotinus remained to the end of his life.

Augustine expresses a strong commitment to free will in his early writings. In *Catholic and Manichean Ways of Life*, he says, rational souls that have fallen away from God still, "possess that immense power of free choice."[4] Throughout his early works he clearly sees free choice as an "immense power," which even fallen humanity possesses. Free choice allows humans to decide whether they will love God or worldly things. It allows them to choose their own character and eternal destiny. Much of his early writing is dedicated to proving free choice of the will to the deterministic Manichees.

In *True Religion*, Augustine insists the rational soul has the capability to contemplate eternal things and obtain eternal life, though it must be helped in this pursuit by grace and "personal illumination" from God.[5] All have the "power to participate in the grace of God," and by choosing to either accept or reject grace, "everyone voluntarily makes himself corn or chaff."[6] The wicked are those who fall away from God by "voluntary defect,"[7] that is, they do so freely of their own choice. For Augustine, sin must be voluntary, since, "one either has to deny that a sin has been committed or to confess that it has been committed willingly."[8] If "sin overtook a man against his will, like a fever, the penalty which follows the

---

4. Augustine, *Catholic and Manichaean Ways of Life*, 7.9.
5. Augustine, *True Religion*, 2.3.
6. Ibid., 6.10.
7. Ibid., 11.21.
8. Ibid., 14.27.

Augustine's Early Works

sinner and is called condemnation would rightly seem to be unjust. But in fact sin is so much a voluntary evil that it is not sin at all unless it is voluntary."[9] He concludes, "Therefore, it is by the will that sin is committed. And since there is no doubt that sins are committed, I cannot see that it can be doubted that souls have free choice in willing. God judged that men would serve him better if they served him freely. That could not be so if they served him by necessity and not by free will."[10]

Thus, according to Augustine, "free will" or "free choice in willing" demands freedom from necessity. When Satan persuaded Adam to sin, Adam's will had to freely consent to Satan's persuasion. "If he had consented by necessity," says Augustine, "he would have been held guilty of no sin."[11] Freedom from necessity remains in Adam's offspring, as well, since "he [God] has given to all the possibility to be good, and has given to all the power to abide in the good as far as they would or could."[12] For Augustine, the will's freedom to choose what it will love, without any necessity being imposed upon it, is essential both for moral responsibility for sin and for the capability to be in a relationship with God, which is characterized by love rather than obligation.

At the end of his life, Augustine wrote a summary of all his works called, *Retractations*, which is Latin for "reconsiderations." In this work he commented on each of his previous works and sometimes revised or reinterpreted them. These revisions reflect his mature theology, not his early theology, but they are important to consider alongside the early works because they show us how Augustine reinterpreted his early works in his later years. In the *Retractations* chapter on *True Religion*, Augustine attempts to reinterpret his statement, "Sin is so voluntary an evil that it is by no means sin if it is not voluntary."[13] By the time he wrote *Retractations*, Augustine believed Adam's descendants sinned necessarily, which in *True Religion*, was the opposite of voluntary. He proposes a revised definition of "voluntary," suggesting that even necessary sins might still be called "voluntary," since they "cannot be committed entirely without the will."[14]

9. Ibid.
10. Ibid.
11. Ibid., 14.28.
12. Ibid., 55.113.
13. Ibid., 14.27.
14. Augustine, *Retractations*, 1.12.5.

The man who is overtaken by sin, "like a fever," can now be justly condemned for that sin because "he yields to concupiscence voluntarily, and, therefore, does only what he wills."[15] Even "original sin in infants, for they do not as yet use free choice of the will, is not improperly called voluntary," he claims, because it was inherited from the first evil will, which did sin voluntarily.[16]

While we may admire Augustine's rhetorical skill with words, many find fault with this drastic redefinition of "voluntary." In *True Religion* "voluntary" means something that one is free to do or not do; to will or not will. It means being free from necessity and having legitimate choice between possibilities. In *Retractations* it simply means any act committed with the will, whether the will was free from necessity or not. Voluntary acts of the will no longer require a free will.

Modern philosophers distinguish between "first-order" and "second-order" volitions of the will to describe the distinction Augustine is making in *Retractations*. In first-order volitions, the will directs some faculty of the body to act. In second-order volitions, the will defines itself. It judges between conflicting first-order volitions and decides whether to say "Yes" or "No" to them. In *True Religion*, both first-order and second-order volitions must be free from obligation or necessity of any kind. In *Retractations*, second-order volitions are overcome and enslaved by lust and have lost the power to choose between good and evil and can only choose evil. Though this means second-order volitions are no longer free, Augustine insists the will remains free and moral responsibility is upheld as long as first-order volitions are free. Sinners compelled by a gun to their head are not considered "free" because their first-order volitions are compelled. However, sinners whose second-order volitions are compelled or necessary are still considered "free." This dramatic shift from an emphasis on the will's freedom to choose what it will love to the acceptance of a predetermined will, which lacks the power to choose what it will love, but is free to act according to the will it has been given, gives us a glimpse of the changes we will see in Augustine's later works. It also helps us to define what we are looking for in his early works. We need to carefully observe what second-order freedoms he ascribes to the will, that is, how free the will is to define itself by choosing what it will love and

---

15. Ibid.
16. Ibid.

Augustine's Early Works

desire. We will also want to understand how he justifies removing these second-order freedoms and accepts the substantially inferior freedom of action as his definition of voluntary willing.

Free Will

Augustine's work entitled *Free Will* offers the clearest presentation of his early doctrines of election, grace, and the will, prior to the seismic shift that occurs when he writes *To Simplician*. Book 1 begins with Augustine's student, Evodius, asking whether God is the cause of evil. Many students of philosophy have wondered, with Evodius, why a good God would allow evil in the world. Some have concluded that God is the author of evil because he is the creator. Augustine seeks to absolve God of responsibility for moral evil by distinguishing between two types of evil: "the evil a man has done, and the evil he has suffered."[17] "God is not the author of the evil a man does," though he may, at times, cause the evil a man suffers, such as natural catastrophes.[18] When Evodius asks who the author of evil not attributed to God is, Augustine insists there is no single author. "Every man is the author of his evil deeds."[19] This is the primary thesis of *Free Will*, as Augustine seeks to prove that God is not the author of the evil men do. Through the voluntary use of his free will, every man is the author of his own evil deeds.

Evodius asks if there is a "cause" of evil doing. Is there something we can blame for our evil deeds? Augustine recommends they first discuss "what doing evil is."[20] Evil is not just an action, he says, but it is also the lust or desire that motivates the action. The wise man uses his mind, reason, or spirit to rule over these desires, which sets him above the beasts who simply act on their strongest desires.[21] "Nothing makes the mind a companion of cupidity [lust], except its own will and free choice."[22] Nothing forces the will "to abandon virtue or to collapse its life into lust."[23]

---

17. Augustine, *Free Will*, 1.1.1.
18. Ibid.
19. Ibid.
20. Ibid., 1.3.6.
21. Ibid., 1.9.19.
22. Ibid., 1.11.21.
23. Babcock, "Sin, Penalty, and the Responsibility of the Soul," 226.

Free to Say No?

Otherwise, sin would be necessary and not culpable. The free will possesses the power to choose whether it will assent to evil impulses or resist them, which means there is no "cause" for man's doing evil but his own choices.

Fallen man exists in a world "dominated by lust," which Augustine calls a penal condition.[24] Evodius understands why Adam is justly punished with this penal condition, since he willingly chose to fall away from God, but he wonders how we, who have never "deserted the fortress of virtue and chosen servitude to lust," can be said to endure this condition deservedly.[25] It is essential to note that most of what follows in the first two books of *Free Will* is Augustine's answer to this question, not a study of Adam's primal condition before the first sin, as he alleges in book 3.

Augustine begins his response by asking Evodius if he has a will. When Evodius wavers, Augustine tells him he would be unable to learn, pursue wisdom, have real friendships, or even be happy if he did not have a will.[26] Evodius admits he has a will, so Augustine asks him if it is a "good will," which "desires to live rightly."[27] When Evodius says it is, Augustine makes some vital remarks, "You see, then, I imagine, that it is in the power of our will to enjoy or to be without so great and so true a good. For what is so completely within the power of the will as the will itself? Whoever has a good will has something which is far better than all earthly realms and all bodily pleasures. Whoever does not have it, lacks that which is more excellent than all the goods which are not in our power, and yet he can have it by willing it simply."[28]

In this critical passage, Augustine establishes that one of the essential characteristics of the will is its power to choose its own disposition. The morally responsible will is free to choose whether it wishes to be a good will or a bad will. "For what is so completely within the power of the will as the will itself?" Nothing is so completely within the power of the will as its freedom to choose its own moral disposition. T. Kermit Scott instructs, "The good will is, for Augustine, the very paradigm of that which is in our power, because it is the one thing that cannot possibly fail to be in our

---

24. Augustine, *Free Will*, 1.11.22.
25. Ibid., 1.12.23–24.
26. Ibid., 1.12.25.
27. Ibid.
28. Ibid., 1.12.26.

power."[29] The point Augustine is making is that fallen man rightly suffers under the dominion of lust, because he does not exercise his power to will to be good. The penal condition he faces after Adam's sin does not annul his ability "to love the good will and hold it in high esteem."[30] When he chooses to not do this, he becomes enslaved to lust.

Augustine's use of the expressions, "we who have never deserted the fortress of virtue" and, "even if we have never been wise formerly," indicate that he is describing the condition of fallen man, who retains power to choose his own character, even in his fallen state. If he chooses to "love and embrace this good will," says Augustine, then virtue dwells in his soul.[31] Evodius rejoices, "I find I can so quickly and so easily obtain so great a good [the good will]."[32] Obviously, he understood their discussion to be about men like himself, not the unique case of Adam. The punishment for Adam's sin makes it more difficult for us to choose good, but it does not render that choice impossible.

Against Manichean determinism, Augustine is arguing that moral responsibility requires that each individual's being good or evil be the consequence of his own free choices. Morally responsible choice must be voluntary, though it may occur in an environment influenced by lust. John Burnaby claims *Free Will* established the ethical point of view, "no action is sin for which the agent cannot be held personally responsible."[33] The will is morally responsible specifically because it is not forced toward any choice, but has "power" to choose between moral alternatives. This power of choice does not mean there are no influences upon the will as it makes its choice, but it does mean these influences do not necessitate any particular choice. Augustine rightly asks, "For what is so completely within the power of the will as the will itself?"[34]

Augustine contends there are two types of men in the world: those who love and pursue eternal things and those who love and pursue temporal things. He concludes book 1 with the important summary, "What each one chooses to pursue and embrace is within the power of his will to

29. Scott, *Augustine*, 161.
30. Augustine, *Free Will*, 1.13.28.
31. Ibid., 1.13.29.
32. Ibid.
33. Burnaby, *Amor Dei*, 186.
34. Augustine, *Free Will*, 1.12.26.

determine. Will alone can drive the mind from the seat of authority and from the right course."[35] This completes their inquiry into "what doing evil means." It is nothing but the will's choice to neglect the eternal and good in order to pursue the temporal and evil. Evodius agrees, "all sins are included in this one class."[36] All sins are voluntary choices of the will. Evodius thinks they have also been successful in answering their second question, "What is the cause of evil doing"? His answer is, "we do it by the free choice of our will."[37] That is to say, there is no cause, external or internal, that is prior to willing and compels the free choice of the will in any direction.

This affirmation of the fallen will's free choice in willing includes the power to choose between good and evil. This is important to note, because in book 3 Augustine will assert that Adam alone had this freedom. He will contend that Adam's descendants lost this freedom after Adam's sin. Babcock rejects this reversal, claiming Augustine's chief aim in writing *Free Will* was to prove to the Manichees, "we are ourselves the fully responsible authors of evil that we do, that our exercise of moral agency in this regard is undiminished and unimpaired . . . The vindication of God, therefore requires a vindication of unimpaired human moral agency in willing and doing of evil."[38] In book 1 of *Free Will*, Augustine insists that the power of free choice exists in Adam and all his descendants, that it must reflect voluntary and uncaused willing, and that it must include choice between good and evil alternatives.

Book 1 ends and book 2 begins with Evodius asking why God gave man free will, since "our sinning is due to it." Since man would not have been able to sin without free will, he wants to know why God gave us "free choice in willing."[39] Augustine agrees man could not have sinned without free will, but says he could not have lived rightly without it either.[40] Man is good "because he can live aright if he chooses to do so."[41] "The will was free not only to live aright but also to sin," writes Augustine.[42] Free will

35. Ibid., 1.16.34
36. Ibid., 1.16.35.
37. Ibid., 1.16.34.
38. Babcock, "Responsibility," 225–6.
39. Augustine, *Free Will*, 2.1.1.
40. Ibid., 2.1.3.
41. Ibid., 2.1.2.
42. Ibid., 2.1.3.

means freedom to choose either moral alternative. Because either choice is possible, we are rightly held morally responsible for our choice. When God judges a sinner, he will ask him, "Why did you not use your free will for the purpose for which I gave it to you, that is, in order to do right"?[43] Free will was given to man so he could choose right, but this freedom also makes it possible for him to choose evil. Augustine concludes, "God, therefore, must have given and ought to have given man free will."[44] It is this power of choice and self-determination which makes it possible for us to live either praiseworthy or blameworthy lives.

Evodius accepts that free will should have been given to man, but wonders why God did not give it in such a way that it could have only been used rightly.[45] This is a fascinating proposal because it is essentially the notion of "free will" that Augustine adopts in his later works. The question leads to a long discussion comparing God's "greater" goods with "intermediate" and "lesser" goods. The will is labeled an "intermediate" good because it can be used for good or evil.[46] Its "aversion" or "conversion," that is, its choice to love unchangeable good or temporal things, must be voluntary and not coerced.[47] Book 2 concludes with Augustine's declaration, "Because that defective movement is voluntary, it is placed within our power. If you fear it, all you have to do is simply not to will it. If you do not will it, it will not exist."[48]

His rejection of the premise that the will should have been given so that it could only be used rightly reaffirms Augustine's conviction that morally responsible choice may not be caused in any way. The good or evil movement of the will must come from the will's own choice and not any causal influence. Free choice of the will provides a sense of security related to our own character and destiny. Augustine asks, "What can be more secure than to live a life where nothing can happen to you which you did not will?" In a world filled with fatalistic fear, he recognizes that moral responsibility is only logical in a world that is neither causally

---

43. Ibid.
44. Ibid.
45. Ibid., 2.2.4.
46. Ibid., 2.18.47.
47. Ibid., 2.18.51—19.53.
48. Ibid., 2.20.54.

determined or arbitrary. We have the assurance that our eternal destinies will be just in light of our free choices.

At the start of book 3, Evodius repeats the question he posed at the conclusion of book 2, "What is the cause of the movement of the will when it turns from the immutable to the mutable good"?[49] In other words, what causes the will to turn away from God to love lesser things? In book 2, Augustine declared that this defective movement must be voluntary, but Evodius wants to be sure he understands exactly what Augustine means by "voluntary" movement which is "within our power." "Because if free will is so given that it has that movement by nature," Evodius argues, "it turns of necessity to mutable goods; and no blame attaches where nature and necessity prevail."[50] Augustine does not disagree with Evodius's statement that "natural" or "necessary" movement is not culpable. In fact, he chides, "you ought to have no doubt that it was not given in that fashion."[51]

Augustine then uses the illustration of a stone which has been thrown and is falling downward to demonstrate the distinction he makes between "natural" movement and "voluntary" movement. He asks if the stone's falling movement is "the motion of the stone"? Evodius admits that it is, but urges that it is the stone's "natural" movement, for which the stone cannot be blamed because it "is compelled by the necessity of its own nature."[52] He further argues that the soul's movement cannot be "natural," like the stone, or it would not be culpable. Augustine wonders why Evodius still doubts this truth and reminds him of their previous discovery, "that the mind can become the slave of lust only by its own will." It cannot be compelled by anything. "If that movement is accounted blameworthy," he states emphatically, "it is not natural but voluntary." What distinguishes these two is "that it is not in the power of the stone to arrest its downward motion."[53] Therefore its movement is natural and not voluntary. The will, on the other hand, is able to stop its downward movement toward sin and evil, so its movement is voluntary.

Augustine is establishing the vital principle that any movement of the soul, which the will is powerless to stop from happening, cannot be

---

49. Ibid., 3.1.1.
50. Ibid.
51. Ibid.
52. Ibid., 3.1.2.
53. Ibid.

called voluntary. Moral responsibility exists only if the will is capable of dissent. Natural inclinations that necessitate the will's movement in a certain direction are not voluntary and do not deserve blame or reward. Augustine then applies this key principle to their own lives, saying, "all useful learning in this matter has its object and value in teaching us to condemn and restrain that movement, and to convert our wills from falling."[54] His use of the personal pronouns "us" and "our," shows that the wills he is discussing are the wills of fallen men, like he and Evodius. Fallen man is only morally responsible for voluntary sin, that is, sin which is not natural, necessary, or that he cannot stop.

This principle is again applied to fallen man in the next paragraph, when Evodius sums up their findings with the immensely important statement, "I know nothing I could call my own if the will by which I will 'yea' or 'nay' is not my own."[55] Evodius has captured the essence of free will in Augustine's early works in this testimonial. The will is the fundamental aspect of the soul where we define our personhood. We choose what we will love and pursue. We set values and priorities and chart the course of our lives. If my "Yes" or "No" at this level of choice is causally determined by nature, punishment, or any other cause, then it is difficult to understand how these choices represent me or my will. I also bear no moral responsibility for choices that are not my own. *Free Will* states unequivocally that the will is not my own if I do not have the power to say "Yes" or "No" to these most fundamental choices.

Some philosophers consider a person to have free will, so long as they are able to act according to the will they have, even if they are not free to choose what that will is. Augustine takes this position in his later works. However, in *Free Will*, the will itself must be free to choose its own loves and desires or it cannot be called "my own." Evodius goes on to say, "unless the movement of the will towards this or that object is voluntary and within our power, a man would not be praiseworthy when he turns to the higher objects nor blameworthy when he turns to the lower objects, using his will like a hinge."[56] There is no moral responsibility for choices of the will which are not voluntary and within our power.

---

54. Ibid.
55. Ibid., 3.1.3.
56. Ibid.

Free to Say No?

Evodius has identified two key aspects of the will's role in shaping our personhood. First, I must have the power to say "Yes" or "No" to what my will loves or it will not represent my personhood. Second, the will functions "like a hinge," which swings between alternate choices before deciding whether to say "Yes" or "No." Some scholars deny that Augustine ever taught the principle of alternate choice, but it appears evident in the passage above. It is hard to understand how a hinge would be an appropriate image of choice that could only swing in one direction. On the other hand, the hinge is an ideal way to illustrate the principle of choice between alternate possibilities. These two factors are especially important because the question under consideration in *Free Will* is, "What is the cause of the movement of the will"? Augustine is insisting there is no prior cause of the will's movement toward either evil or good. Free from any determining causes, the will considers alternative loves and chooses whether to say "Yes" or "No" to them.

Book 3 of *Free Will* argues against the possibility that corrupted human nature is the cause of evil willing. The will opens the door for the corruption of the nature and not vice versa. "If a nature is corrupted by another's fault and not by its own, it is unjust to blame it,"[57] says Augustine. A virtuous man's nature cannot be corrupted, "unless it is willing to be corrupted. If it is willing, the corruption starts with its own vice and not with the vice of the other."[58] These statements disavow the notion that fallen man's nature has been corrupted by Adam's sin. The corruption of our nature must start with our own voluntary choice and not the vice of another.

Then, even after a nature allows itself to be corrupted by sin, it still retains significant freedom of choice. Augustine asks, "what debt sinful nature owes"? His answer is, "Right action," because "From God it [sinful nature] received the power to act rightly when it would. From him also it received the alternatives, misery if it acts unrighteously, happiness if it acts righteously."[59] Augustine is describing the "sinful nature" of fallen man, not the condition of Adam and Eve before the fall. He says this sinful nature maintains the power to choose good and act righteously. "There is no guilt if they are what they are because they did not receive

57. Ibid., 3.13.38.
58. Ibid., 3.14.39.
59. Ibid., 3.15.43.

power to have an ampler existence."⁶⁰ "No man is guilty because he has not received this or that power," says Augustine, "But because he does not do as he ought he is justly held guilty. Obligation arises if he has received free will and sufficient power."⁶¹ Guilt and moral obligation require the power to choose good. "Because they have the power to be good there is guilt if they will not,"⁶² Augustine concludes. If the will is incapacitated so that it cannot will good, then it sins necessarily and is not guilty of sin. Augustine writes succinctly, "If 'oughtness' depends upon what has been given, and if man has been so made that he sins by necessity, then he ought to sin. So when he sins he does what he ought. But it is wicked to speak like that. No man's nature compels him to sin, nor does any other nature . . . He sinned in that he did something voluntarily . . . So, if no one is compelled to sin either by his own nature or by another, it remains that he sins by his own will."⁶³

It would be hard to state his conclusions any more clearly than, "No man's nature compels him to sin, nor does any other nature." In case the point is missed, however, Augustine entreats, "But what cause of willing can there be that is prior to willing"?⁶⁴ He answers, "Either, then, will is itself the first cause of sin, or the first cause is without sin. Now sin is rightly imputed only to that which sins, nor is it rightly imputed unless it sins voluntarily."⁶⁵ "Whatever be the cause of willing," he continues, "if it cannot be resisted no sin results from yielding to it."⁶⁶ Then, for emphasis he reiterates, no one "commits sin in doing what there was no means avoiding."⁶⁷ In the strongest language possible, Augustine has underscored the absolute necessity for the will to be able to say "Yes" or "No" to sin. Being free to only say "Yes," removes obligation, guilt, and moral responsibility because sin cannot be resisted or avoided.

At the end of book 3, we find a dramatic shift in Augustine's understanding of man's fallen condition. Many scholars believe this portion of *Free Will* was written several years after he wrote the previous sections.

60. Ibid., 3.15.44.
61. Ibid. 3.15.45.
62. Ibid., 3.15.44.
63. Ibid., 3.16.46.
64. Ibid. 3.17.49.
65. Ibid.
66. Ibid., 3.18.50.
67. Ibid.

Chadwick claims *Free Will* was authored over a period of six or seven years.[68] Babcock asserts that during the seven years he was writing *Free Will*, "Augustine's thinking on moral agency underwent developments that put his own claims at risk."[69] Robert Evans contends, the dialogue in the three books of *Free Will*, "is a work that is at unity neither with itself nor with the later and more developed theology of its author."[70] The discontinuity becomes most evident near the end of book 3, when Augustine claims the freedom he has been describing previously in *Free Will* was only found in man as he was created. Fallen man, he says, "has not the freedom of will to choose to do what he ought to do or fulfill it when he will."[71] He is beset by ignorance and difficulty, which were "not in the nature of man as he was made, but are the penalties of man who has been condemned."[72] Pointing to Paul's struggle with sin in Rom. 7:18–19, Augustine explains, "Wrong things are done by necessity when a man wills to do right and has not the power."[73] Fallen man, he concludes, "is not good, nor is it in his power to become good."[74] Free will was lost because Adam was unwilling to use it properly when he could.[75]

Augustine's elimination of fallen man's freedom to do good is a reversal of his early teaching. His contention, "the freedom of the will to do right" he had been discussing was intended only to apply to Adam's condition before the fall, seems disingenuous considering how frequently his previous discussions ascribed this freedom to the "sinful nature," "any man," and "every man." In fact, some of his most important teachings on the will's freedom to do good in book 1 revolved around those "who certainly are foolish and were never wise." This is a reference to fallen man and the conclusions he reached ought to be applied to fallen man. He and Evodius certainly applied their conclusions to their own wills on several occasions. Babcock believes that Augustine is attempting "to

---

68. Chadwick, *Augustine: Short Introduction*, 40.
69. Babcock, "Responsibility," 227.
70. Evans, *Pelagius*, 86.
71. Augustine, *Free Will*, 3.18.52.
72. Ibid.
73. Ibid., 3.18.51.
74. Ibid.
75. Ibid., 3.18.52.

draw the consequences of his new position"[76] and reinterpret his previous statements.

What led Augustine to make such a radical change? Some scholars propose it was a consequence of his debate with Fortunatus in 392.[77] On the first day of this debate, Augustine firmly insists, "someone who is forced by necessity to do something does not sin."[78] On the second day he repeats, "I say there is no sin if we do not sin by our own will, and for this reason there is also a reward, because we act rightly by our own will."[79] However, when Fortunatus quotes Romans 7 to show man is sometimes incapable of doing what he wills, Augustine retreats to the position, "free choice of the will existed in the man who was first created . . . But after he sinned by free will, we who are descended from his stock were cast down into necessity."[80]

Babcock says, Augustine gives habit (*consuetudo*) "the force of necessity" for the first time in this debate and consequently from now on he has to restrict the exercise of the free will to the first man.[81] Yet, as Babcock notes, this absence of free will is the result of "habit" or continued practice of sin. Through habitual sinning, man becomes enslaved to sin and loses his free will. Augustine argues in this debate, that necessity comes only after man has yielded to sin by "free choice." Habitual yielding to sin leads to necessity, but we do not sin necessarily from birth. Before we become entangled in a sinful habit, Augustine asserts, "we have in our actions the free choice of doing or not doing something."[82] The free choice of doing or not doing something is the freedom to say "Yes" or "No" to good or evil alternatives. Without this freedom there is no moral choice. This freedom can be surrendered by a habitually yielding to sin, but as a result of free choice. His contention in book 3 of *Free Will*, that fallen man has lost freedom of will to choose to do good, appears to be more radical than the position he defended in the *Debate with Fortunatus*.

---

76. Babcock, "Responsibility," 228.
77. Ibid., 229.
78. Augustine, *Debate with Fortunatus*, 17.
79. Ibid., 21.
80. Ibid., 22.
81. Babcock, "Moral Agency," 39–40.
82. Augustine, *Fortunatus*, 22.

Free to Say No?

Wetzel comments on Augustine's radical change, when he writes, "A more dramatic departure from book 1 of *De libero arbitrio* (*Free Will*) could hardly be imagined."[83] Just prior to introducing this twist in book 3, Augustine had demanded, "But what cause of willing can there be which is prior to willing"? His answer was, "Either, then, will is itself the first cause of sin, or the first cause is without sin."[84] He was adamant, "Whatever be the cause of willing, if it cannot be resisted no sin results from yielding."[85] If original sin has now become the "cause" of all sin which follows the primal sin, then Adam's sin alone will meet the criteria to be called "sin."

Augustine quickly responds to objections, "They say: If Adam and Eve sinned, what have we miserable creatures done to deserve to be born in the darkness of ignorance and in the toils of difficulty?"[86] His opponents appear to be asking a question similar to what Evodius asked in book 1, but Augustine's response is dramatically different this time around. His initial reply is a caustic, "Keep quiet and stop murmuring against God."[87] However, he then admits his opponents might have a valid complaint, if man had been left in this condition without any aid available. Man is not guilty because of his penal condition, he says, but rather because he refuses to avail himself of the aid that is available to him in this penal state.[88] He assures us that God is willing to heal all who will humbly accept his aid, "But if any of Adam's race should be willing to turn to God, and so overcome that punishment which had been merited by the original turning away from God, it was fitting not only that he should not be hindered, but that he should also receive divine aid. In this way also the Creator showed how easily man might have retained, if he had so willed, the nature with which he was created, because his offspring had power to transcend that in which he was born."[89]

In this passage, fallen man is not totally incapacitated by sin, but has power to overcome his penal condition by willing to turn to God

---

83. Wetzel, *Virtue*, 397.
84. Augustine, *Free Will*, 3.17.49.
85. Ibid., 3.18.50.
86. Ibid., 3.19.53.
87. Ibid.
88. Ibid.
89. Ibid., 3.20.55.

and accept his aid. Babcock explains, "ignorance and difficulty do not unjustly burden the soul, so that even in our impaired condition, we retain a restricted, but not negligible, capacity for moral agency."[90] He believes Augustine carved out a narrow, but crucial area of moral agency for fallen man in *Free Will*, though he concedes that Augustine eventually discards this position.[91]

The end of book 3 clarifies Augustine's evolving view of the relationship between grace and free will prior to the writing of *To Simplician*. By claiming the "freedom of the will to do right" belonged only to Adam, he clearly disavows the Pelagian view of the will, which claimed the fallen will was unaffected by Adam's sin. Yet, he does not negate all freedom of choice for the fallen will. It sometimes lacks knowledge of what is right, but it remains free to seek that knowledge. It is able to will what is good, though it may lack the power to do the good it wills. Ultimately, the fallen will retains the power to choose to be a good will or a bad will, as Augustine had taught in book 1. Even at the end of book 3, he says, sinful souls have the "natural power" to discern wisdom from error and seek good things.[92] Though born in ignorance and difficulty, they are under no necessity to remain in that state.[93]

Augustine's denial of the "freedom of the will to do right" in Adam's descendants is not yet a denial of all freedom to will the good, but only the denial of unrestrained freedom. The fallen will remains free to exercise its choice between good and evil, even under the penal influences of difficulty and ignorance. These penalties impede the freedom to choose good, but they do not eliminate it. Augustine also denies original guilt on numerous occasions, saying the blame for these penal conditions, "is ascribed neither to the souls nor to their Creator."[94] He assures us ignorance and difficulty are only the starting point for the soul's progress. The freedom to choose to progress remains in the power of the will, "for the capacity to do so is not denied to it."[95] Three times, he says, this penal condition is "natural" to man, then insists that "no one rightly blames him for

---

90. Babcock, "Responsibility," 230.
91. Ibid.
92. Augustine, *Free Will*, 3.20.56.
93. Ibid.
94. Ibid., 3.20.57.
95. Ibid., 3.22.64.

the natural condition from which he started."⁹⁶ As in the first two books of *Free Will*, there is no moral responsibility for "natural" or "necessary" sin, so the will must retain power to will good and say "No" to sin.

Augustine has increased his emphasis on the fallen will's need for grace. It is unable to overcome ignorance and difficulty without this aid. But he assures his readers that grace will be given, "if it [the will] makes a good use of what it has received. It has received the power to seek diligently and piously if it will."⁹⁷ He even praises God for having given the fallen soul "so good a start" and "so much dignity as to put within its power the capacity to grow towards happiness if it will."⁹⁸ He summarizes, "So man has imposed on him a penalty which was corrective rather than destructive."⁹⁹

It is important to note what Augustine has not done at the end of book 3. He has not eliminated the fallen will's freedom to turn to God to receive grace. He has not ascribed to the will the total subservience to sin or the penal guilt that we see him professing in his later works. Carol Harrison comments, "human beings are not held guilty for Adam's sin, even though they justly suffer the punishment for it, but they are guilty if they fail to confess their weakness humbly and to acknowledge their absolute helplessness, ignorance and need for God's healing grace."¹⁰⁰

If fallen man does not acknowledge his need for grace, he will be overcome by ignorance and difficulty, and will become enslaved to sin. On the other hand, if he humbly accepts God's grace, he will find God's healing power freely available to him.¹⁰¹ The choice between these two alternatives remains in the power of the will, which retains the essential powers of assent and dissent. That is, it has the freedom of choice to say "Yes" or "No" to its own sinful inclinations, as well as to God's offer of grace.

In *Retractations*, Augustine explains "grace" was only mentioned in passing, but not defended by laborious reasoning in *Free Will*, because

---

96. Ibid.
97. Ibid., 3.22.65.
98. Ibid.
99. Ibid., 3.25.76.
100. Harrison, *Rethinking*, 218.
101. Ibid., 223.

it was not the subject under discussion.[102] He also notes that he did not explain in *Free Will*, the way God prepares the wills of his elect. While he admits to his many statements about the voluntary nature of sin and his requirement that nothing can be the cause of the will, in *Retractations*, he contends these statements are only true of the will "freed by the grace of God."[103] He acknowledges having written that intermediate goods, like the will, can be used "not only rightly, but also wrongly," but reminds us he also wrote, "The virtues by which man lives rightly are great goods," which cannot be used wrongly.[104]

In this last statement, he is claiming to have taught that the ability to use the will rightly was a virtue which came only as a gift of God. This claim appears inconsistent with the way he presented both the will and virtue in *Free Will*. The quote he presents came in his response to Evodius' suggestion that the free will should have been given in such a way that it could only be used rightly. Augustine clearly disagreed with Evodius' suggestion and insisted the "aversion" or "conversion" of the will must be voluntary and not coerced.[105] The will's movement toward good or evil has to be a voluntary movement. On virtue, he taught, "A man is made virtuous by regulating his soul according to the rules and guiding lights of the virtues."[106] He also taught, "The will . . . obtains man's first and best good things [like virtue] though it is itself only an intermediate good."[107] Finally, he claims, "If we love and embrace this good will, those virtues . . . which together constitute right and honourable living, dwell in our souls."[108] Virtue is described as a guiding light for the will's choices. It is a goal to be obtained by the will's choices. It is never described as the force that drives or motivates the will's choices. Augustine disallowed this type of causal influence on the will, so that it could only be used rightly, when he responded to Evodius' proposition that God should have made the will this way. He insisted that the will's movements toward either good or evil must be voluntary and not coerced by any cause, internal or external.[109]

102. Augustine, *Retractations*, 1.8.2.
103. Ibid., 1.8.2–3.
104. Ibid., 1.8.4.
105. Augustine, *Free Will*, 2.18.51–19.53.
106. Ibid., 2.18.52.
107. Ibid., 2.18.53.
108. Ibid., 1.13.29.
109. Ibid., 2.13.47.

Free to Say No?

We conclude our study of *Free Will* by looking at one last issue found in book 3, which troubles many who believe in both free will and God's foreknowledge. Evodius asks if God's foreknowledge causes sin to be necessary.[110] He wonders if God's foreknowing an event means that event cannot happen other than he has foreknown it. Augustine is not nearly as bothered by this concern as Evodius was, or as some modern day scholars are. He explains, God has foreknowledge because he "foresees what all men are going to will in the future."[111] Foreknowledge does not preclude the action of will or God himself would have to act out of necessity and not freely.[112] He asserts, "Therefore, there is nothing so much in our power as the will itself . . . We can rightly say that we do not grow old voluntarily but necessarily, or that we do not die voluntarily but from necessity . . . But who but a raving fool would say that it is not voluntarily that we will?"[113]

He distinguishes between necessity, which includes things we are powerless to change, and those events that are a result of the will's choices. If I must necessarily will something because God foreknows it, he says, "it must be admitted that I will, not voluntarily but from necessity."[114] He assumes there is a difference "between things that happen according to God's foreknowledge where there is no intervention of man's will at all, and things that happen because of a will of which he has foreknowledge."[115] He calls the notion, "I must necessarily so will," a "monstrous assertion," and asks, "If I must necessarily will, why need I speak of willing at all?"[116] He concludes, "Our will would not be will unless it were in our power. Because it is in our power, it is free."[117]

Augustine's resolution of the problem of foreknowledge is to recognize that God has contingent knowledge of our wills, but "in such a way that our wills remain free and within our power."[118] T. Kermit Scott says, "people confuse knowing that something will happen and causing

110. Ibid., 3.2.4.
111. Ibid., 3.3.6.
112. Ibid.
113. Ibid., 3.3.7.
114. Ibid., 3.3.8.
115. Ibid.
116. Ibid.
117. Ibid.
118. Ibid.

it to happen."[119] God has foreknowledge of all that will happen, "but is not the agent of all that he foreknows."[120] He foreknows that we will have power over our own wills and not be compelled by any force, not even his foreknowledge.

After Free Will

In *Two Souls*, written around 392, Augustine argues against the determinism of the Manichees. He condemns their heresy based on two principles: his definition of the will and his definition of sin.[121] The will is defined as, "a movement of the soul, with nothing forcing it."[122] It is "obvious everywhere and available to all," he declares, a person who is willing is free from being forced. "Unwilling is the contrary to willing," so that "every one who does something unwillingly is forced, and everyone who is forced does it unwillingly."[123] Sin is defined as, "the will to retain or to acquire what justice forbids and from which one is free to hold back."[124] From these definitions, we see that "will" and "sin" both require freedom from necessity. Sin cannot exist without the will and the will that is not free, "is not a will," says Augustine.[125]

He assures us he did not have to examine rare books to arrive at these definitions, since they are known by shepherds, poets, teachers, priests, and even the unlearned on the street corners. These definitions and the principle of freedom from compulsion are understood and affirmed by all. It is important to note that both of these definitions include the power of dissent. Augustine states, "There is sin when we will what is unjust and are free not to will it."[126] Freedom to not will something is essential to Augustine's early concept of free will.

To illustrate the relationship between the will and sin, Augustine proposes four hypothetical persons. The first, is someone asleep, whose

---

119. Scott, *Augustine*, 167.
120. Augustine, *Free Will*, 3.4.11.
121. Augustine, *Two Souls*, 12.16.
122. Ibid., 10.14.
123. Ibid.
124. Ibid., 11.15.
125. Ibid.
126. Ibid.

hand is used by another to do evil. Everyone denies this is sin because there is no exercise of the will. The second, is someone bound and restrained, who is caused to do evil by another. This person is also not guilty of sin because he was forced to sin. The third person drinks himself to sleep, so that another may use him to do evil. This person is guilty of sin because he willingly made himself available for this purpose. The fourth person lets himself be bound willingly, so that his members may be used for sin. He is also guilty of sin because he also willingly made himself available for evil. The conclusion Augustine draws is, "sin exists nowhere but in the will."[127] His examples show free will may not be required at the moment a sinful act is committed for it to be culpable. However, at some point prior to the sinful action, the will must have freely chosen to allow itself to be used for evil. If there was never freedom to say "No," then there is no sin.

Robert Kane presents an outstanding argument for why the will must have "ultimate responsibility" for its choices and cannot be predetermined, in his book, *The Significance of Free Will*.[128] Kane suggests a person might come to wholeheartedly will something by brainwashing, or being manipulated by a cult leader, or being given a mind-altering drug, and might even be satisfied with his will, yet "would lack autonomy in the deeper sense of 'control over our own wills' that was traditionally associated with free will."[129] He proposes that there are two kinds of control which may be exercised over a person. The first is "constraining control," when someone is forced to do something against his will by a threat of harm or punishment. The person may be held at gunpoint, threatened with blackmail, or compelled by other "constraining" influences. The second, which Kane calls, "nonconstraining control," is when someone's will is manipulated so it wants and desires only what it has been causally determined to will. The person may not even be aware their will has been manipulated. They act "freely" according to their own wants and desires, but they did not freely choose those wants and desires.[130]

One example of nonconstraining control is found in B. F. Skinner's *Walden Two*. In the story, all the people in this utopian community are

---

127. Ibid., 10.12.
128. Kane, *Significance*, 60–78.
129. Ibid., 64.
130. Ibid., 64–65.

Augustine's Early Works

conditioned from birth to want and choose only what the leaders allow them to want and choose. They are said to be completely "free" because they do whatever they want. Yet, as Kane notes, most readers would not agree that the inhabitants of Walden Two are "free," since their wills are not their own.[131] The early Augustine would have agreed with this analysis. He insisted the will itself must be "in our power." The later Augustine, however, would have affirmed the free will of the citizens of Walden Two, because they acted according to their own wills and their actions were "voluntary." In *Free Will* he argues that a person must be free to will or not will something. In other words, he must bear ultimate responsibility for what his will wants. If he is manipulated by some external force so that he wills what the external force causes him to want, with no freedom to not will it, then his will is not his own, it is not a will, and it is not free. Causation negates willing because willing presupposes voluntary movement that is free from necessity.

Augustine asserts that anyone who accepts the definitions of "will" and "sin" he proposes in *Two Souls* finds the whole case of the Manichees brought to an end. Passionately he claims, "it is the height of injustice and insanity to hold someone guilty of sin because he did not do what he could not do."[132] He resolves, "Hence, whatever those souls do, if they do it by nature and not by will, that is, if they lack the free movement of the soul both to do it and not to do it, and if, finally, they are given no ability to refrain from their action, we cannot maintain any sin on their part."[133] He calls the will a "neutral entity," which considers good and bad options, then assents to one or the other after wavering back and forth between the two options.[134]

In *Retractations*, Augustine rejects these definitions from *Two Souls*. He points to Paul's wrestling with sins that were against his will and asks, "How, then, is there never sin but in the will"? He says his definition of "will" in *Two Souls* remains valid only when it is applied to the first couple in paradise, who were under no compulsion when they sinned with free will.[135] He also claims his definition of "sin" was only appropriate for

---

131. Ibid., 65.
132. Augustine, *Two Souls*, 12.17.
133. Ibid.
134. Ibid., 13.19.
135. Augustine, *Retractations*, 1.14.3.

defining the original sin of Adam, not the sins of his descendants, who are "under the domination of passion," and have wills that are "corrupt and subject to sin."[136] Fallen man is now judged guilty of sin, though he lacks the free movement of the will to not do it. As to his allegation in *Two Souls* that "it was the height of injustice and insanity to hold someone guilty of sin because he did not do what he could not do," Augustine now justifies our guilt for sin we can not avoid as our punishment for Adam's sin. "For what is every man on earth by origin but Adam?"[137] Even infants are born guilty before committing any sin because of their origin in Adam.[138] The only way he can maintain his definitions from *Two Souls* is to limit them to defining Adam's will and sin, while suggesting the will and sin of Adam's descendants are of an entirely different nature.

About the same time he wrote *Two Souls*, Augustine had his famous debate with Fortunatus. During this debate, he explains, "Since, then, we were to be good not by necessity but by will, God had to give free choice to the soul."[139] This is a claim found throughout his early works. He believes God gave man free will, because he did not want to be served by necessity, but by man's free choice. In disputing the Manichean view, which says we sin by necessity, he argues that the soul in such a condition would rightly cry out, "I have lost my free choice. You know the necessity that has pressed me down. Why do you blame me for the wounds I received?"[140] He completely rejects this Manichean view, "For someone who does not sin by his will does not sin."[141] When Fortunatus asks him what the origin of sin was, he replies, "I say that there is no sin if we do not sin by our own will . . . Since, then, you recognize the necessity by which I was overwhelmed . . . which I could not resist, why do you accuse me as a sinner?"[142]

In *Retractations*, Augustine says he had intended these statements to apply only to "that sin which is not also a punishment for sin."[143] That is to say, these assertions that moral responsibility only exists where choice is

---

136. Ibid., 1.14.4.
137. Ibid., 1.14.5.
138. Ibid., 1.14.6.
139. Augustine, *Debate with Fortunatus*, 15.
140. Ibid., 17.
141. Ibid., 20.
142. Ibid., 21.
143. Augustine, *Retractations*, 1.15.2.

Augustine's Early Works

free from necessity, should only be applied to Adam. His descendants sin necessarily as a punishment for Adam's sin. Wetzel says of this disclaimer, "Augustine seems to have cut his losses on the problems surrounding voluntary sin by excluding it from the fallen world."[144] Babcock observes, "he has now restricted the free exercise of the will to the first instance, the first sin of the first human being."[145] No sin after Adam's was committed with free will. The only difference between his position in *Retractations* and the position of Fortunatus during the debate is that he regards Adam's sin as the cause for humanity's descent into necessity, rather than the "nation of darkness" blamed by the Manichees. Babcock concludes, Augustine "never quite managed to shed his Manichean past."[146]

This brings us to the end of Augustine's early works, in which he has staked out a strong position in defense of free will. Election is God's recognition of those, who by their own free will have chosen to receive his gracious offer of salvation. All have the power to participate in God's grace and all who hear the gospel have within their will the freedom to decide whether to be corn or chaff. The fallen human will has the power to say "Yes" or "No" to sinful impulses and to grace.

Augustine's belief in free will is unquestionable in the early works. Sarah Byers notes how he interchanged *voluntas* (will) and *libera voluntas* (free will), so that *libera* served to emphasize the free nature of the will.[147] Yet, exactly what he meant by "free will" remains the subject of some debate. Karen Rogers claims Augustine was a "consistent compatibilist."[148] She points to his insistence in *Retractations* that the Pelagians had misunderstood his teaching in *Free Will*. If he was a libertarian, she contends, he would have been "misrepresenting" his early work.[149] Some scholars believe this is exactly what Augustine did in his later works, as his view of "free will" drastically changed from the libertarian position we have documented in his early works to the compatibilist view noted by Rogers in his later works.

---

144. Wetzel, *Virtue*, 97.
145. Babcock, "Moral Agency," 40.
146. Ibid., 30.
147. Byers, "The Meaning of *Voluntas*," 186.
148. Rogers, "Augustine's Compatibilism," 426.
149. Ibid., 423.

Free to Say No?

One of the goals of this book is to evaluate whether Augustine was in fact, a compatibilist when he wrote his early works, or a libertarian, who later abandoned his early notions of "free will." To do this, we will need to briefly define these two philosophical positions. Rogers claims Augustine was a compatibilist because, "He holds that although the causes of human choices are ultimately traceable to factors outside of the agent, this is compatible with the agents being fully responsible for their choices."[150] According to Lynne Baker, compatibilists believe a will can be caused, yet still be free, so long as it is not caused by coercion.[151] A libertarian, on the other hand, does not believe freedom or moral responsibility is compatible with a causally determined will. They believe morally responsible choice must originate with the responsible agent. Libertarian freedom also usually requires alternate possibilities, at least somewhere in the history of the choice. It believes the will is the starting point of human personality, so that it cannot be determined in advance and still be considered "free." There is little doubt Augustine was a compatibilist in his later years, but we have observed how his early works defend a libertarian notion of the will, which requires the will to be the ultimate determiner of its own disposition. In his early works, the will must be free to choose between good and evil second-order volitions and also the first-order alternatives of doing or not doing an action. The will must be free to choose what it wills, not just what it does. These teachings are not consistent with compatibilism.

Throughout his early works, Augustine continually insists that the will is not coerced or compelled to sin. Libertarians and compatibilists would both agree with this condition. His libertarian perspective is revealed in his requirement that the will have the power to choose its own disposition. For Augustine, "*Voluntas* [will] is impulse rooted in the rational capacity of assent to impressions."[152] In *Free Will*, the will is enticed to take action by things it perceives, and though man has no power to control the things he perceives, "It is in a man's power to take or reject this or that."[153] These perceptions are of both superior (eternal) and inferior (temporal) things, but "the rational creature may take from either what it

---

150. Ibid., 415.
151. Baker, "Why Christians," 2.
152. Byers, "Meaning of *Voluntas*," 185.
153. Augustine, *Free Will*, 3.25.74.

will."[154] The will gives man the rational capacity to choose which perceptions to assent to or dissent from. Byers says, "to be rational is to have the capacity to yield or not yield to impressions."[155] The compatibilist will has only the power to assent or yield to impressions, it does not have the power to dissent from them. It does not choose its own disposition.

Augustine's teaching, that the will is always moved by what it desires is consistent with a compatibilist view, but his emphasis on the will's freedom to choose which desires it will assent to or dissent from is not. John DePoe explains, compatibilism claims a person's free choice is caused by "effective desires," which have been caused by God.[156] For that reason, dissent from these "effective desires" is not possible. Augustine's early view of the will as a hinge or neutral entity, which is not irresistibly drawn in any direction but is free to choose between the alternate possibilities of good and evil, is a libertarian perspective. As we saw in *Retractations*, he came to deny the will's ability to dissent from lust and choose good, but in the early works he affirms free choice in willing good or evil and ferociously argues against the idea of a will which is determined by anything but its own choices.

Rogers argues that Augustine's early view of the will did not entail "open options."[157] She says, compatibilism maintains the will is free because it acts according to its own disposition, even if it is never free to say "No" to the moral disposition it has been given. This was not the free will that Augustine defended in his early works. He rejected any cause of the will prior to the will's own choices. If the will's loves and desires are imposed upon it by a cause external to the self, then, he says, the will is not free and is not even a will. The will must be free to choose whether or not it will assent to various loves and desires that present themselves. Effective desires that cause the will's necessary choice, remove freedom and moral responsibility.

Assent is an important constituent of *voluntas*. Rist defines *voluntas* as, "a love which has been accepted or consented to."[158] The will must be free to choose what loves or desires it will accept, assent or consent

---

154. Ibid.
155. Byers, "Meaning of *Voluntas*," 186.
156. DePoe, "Why Christians Should Not Be Compatibilists," 1.
157. Rogers, "Compatibilism," 424.
158. Rist, *Augustine: Ancient Thought Baptized*, 176–7.

to. Freely choosing to assent implies the freedom to dissent as well. Rist notes, the phrase "free will" (*libera voluntas*) occurs rarely before Augustine, suggesting it might be his alternative for the more common phrase "free choice of the will" (*liberum arbitrium voluntatis*).[159] This would imply, the phrase "free will" contains the notion of a will, which has free choice and is not simply driven by its desires. The will judges between desires and decides whether to accept or reject them. Compatibilism, on the other hand, claims God determines each person's desires and then causes them to assent to these desires. The person chooses to assent to these desires without ever having the power to dissent from them. The libertarian concludes that this makes God the ultimate determiner of all "free choices."[160] This is not the notion of will presented by Augustine in his early works.

Byers claims, when Cicero uses the phrase *libera voluntas*, "he presents questions of whether any action is 'of will' (*voluntatis*) as identical to the questions (a) whether anything is in our power (*in nostra potestate*), and (b) whether assent (*assensio*) is in our power."[161] In his early works, Augustine agrees with Cicero that the will has to be in our power and its assent also has to be in our power. Byers says, "since assent is by definition a choice between options (to approve or not approve an impression), it is therefore necessarily free."[162] The power of assent requires the power of dissent or there is no choice. The will must have freedom to will or refrain from willing something, as well as freedom to do or refrain from doing something.

The essential question, then, is whether Augustine taught that the will had only the power of assent or acquiescence, as the Stoics taught,[163] or the more significant libertarian power of choosing between assent and dissent? In his early works, Augustine clearly argues for this more significant level of freedom. It is a freedom which allows the will the power to choose between moral alternatives and decide its own disposition.[164] If the will is not free to resist the downward pull of sin and turn to God

---

159. Ibid, 186.
160. Hamilton, "Philosophical Reflections," 4.
161. Byers, "Meaning of *Voluntas*," 189.
162. Ibid., 184.
163 .Springstead, "Will and Order," 80.
164. Augustine, *Free Will*, 1.12.26.

for aid, then, the will is not in our power and is neither free nor a will.[165] Marianne Djuth suggests John Cassian and Faustus of Riez both rejected Augustine's later positions because they believed the will had the power of both assent and dissent. They argued that, "the will would be subject to coercive force of necessity," if it was not free to dissent from "the weight of carnal concupiscence and the divine offer to remove it."[166]

The will's freedom to say "Yes" or "No" is essential to Augustine's early understanding of sin. Sin must be deliberate and voluntary. If it is not committed willingly, it is not sin. Adam's will had to consent to Satan's persuasion to be guilty of sin. He would not have been guilty, says Augustine, if he had consented by necessity.[167] Sin cannot overtake a man like a fever but must be yielded to freely. The will must be the first cause of any movement toward sin. It cannot be like a stone, which cannot stop its downward movement. It cannot be compelled by the necessity of its own nature. It is like a hinge, which can freely move either direction and say either "Yes" or "No" to evil.

This power of assent or dissent is also essential to Augustine's concept of moral responsibility. God gave man free will because he preferred to have man be good by choice, rather than by necessity.[168] His arguments from *Two Souls* assert that, "willing" and "forced" are contradictory conditions. For man to be morally responsible, his choices must be free and not forced. In our human justice systems, we do not judge someone guilty of a crime if they were powerless to avoid it. Augustine avows that God's justice system also does not punish powerlessness or necessary sin. Actions are right or wrong, and punishment and reward make sense only if there is the power to say "No."[169]

Augustine originally accepted Cicero's reasoning that if an impression is the cause of impulse, assent, or action, then these are not in our power and there is no justice in reward or punishment.[170] That is to say, if an impression causes either assent or action and there is no moment when we choose freely whether to assent to or dissent from the impres-

---

165. Ibid., 3.3.8.
166. Djuth, "Stoicism," 394.
167. Augustine, *True Religion*, 14.28.
168. Augustine, *Debate with Fortunatus*, 15.
169. Augustine, *Free Will*, 2.1.3.
170. Byers, "*Voluntas*," 184.

sion, then we are no more morally responsible than animals following their natural desires. The presence of punishment proves that the soul had freedom to choose to assent or act other than it did. At the judgment, God will ask guilty souls why they did not use their free will to do right, as he had intended.[171] Guilt exists when there is the power to will or act rightly.[172] For Augustine, free will, sin, and moral responsibility all demand freedom of both assent and dissent and not just freedom of assent or acquiescence.

This power of assent or dissent is also a key component of our personhood. As Evodius argued, it would be difficult to know who I am or what can be called "mine," if even the very assent or dissent of my will is not under my own control.[173] Eric Springstead says, "If Augustine sees the will as a matter of deciding between possibilities, the most important choice is accepting or rejecting a certain view of the self and its relation to the world and God." He continues, "What makes that choice crucial for Augustine is that it is this consent that determines the moral quality of the will and person."[174] Springstead adds, "for Augustine, the will, together with the memory and intelligence, is not simply something we have; it is us."[175] For a rational soul to have true personhood, they must have power to choose their own loves and desires. Otherwise, they are nothing more than an irrational animal, which follows its strongest desires. Human personality encompasses the notion that we choose who we are by saying "Yes" or "No" to various moral influences and we are then responsible for the character of the person we become as a result of these choices.

Rogers labels Augustine a compatibilist, even during his early years, because she believes he does not make an argument for the alternative possibilities of choosing either good or evil.[176] This chapter has shown that Augustine does, in fact, frequently make this argument. He describes his own will as a "neutral entity," which considers good and bad options, then assents to one or the other.[177] He insists that sin requires freedom to

---

171. Augustine, *Free Will*, 2.1.3.
172. Ibid., 3.15.44.
173. Ibid., 3.1.3.
174. Springstead, "Order and Will," 82.
175. Ibid., 84.
176. Rogers, "Compatibilism," 424.
177. Augustine, *Two Souls*, 13.19.

hold back, refrain, stop and even not will to sin.[178] Voluntary action demands, "free movement of the soul both to do it [sin] and not to do it."[179] The will considers good and bad options, then assents to one or the other, after wavering back and forth between two options.[180] These are but a few of the instances where Augustine mandated that the will have the alternate possibilities of assent and dissent. For these reasons, we must reject Rogers's contention that Augustine was a compatibilist in his early years, and prefer Djuth's appraisal, that his understanding of human freedom before 396 was not consistent with his later view. He initially defended a libertarian view of the will, but later switched to a compatibilist view, which denied the power of dissent.

Simon Harrison believes that all of Augustine's discussions in book 3, "are simply elaborations on the conclusion reached at the end of book 2: there is no cause (of evil) 'behind the will.'"[181] Even under the penal conditions of ignorance and difficulty, the fallen will has the freedom to choose whether it will say "Yes" or "No" to both good and evil.[182]

---

178. Ibid., 11.15.
179. Ibid., 12.17.
180. Ibid., 13.19.
181. Harrison, *Augustine's Way Into the Will*, 99.
182. Ibid., 60.

Chapter 2

Augustine's Middle Works

In Augustine's middle works we see a progressive shift toward his mature doctrines of grace and election. He was engaged in an intense study of the Epistles of Paul, which darkened his Platonic view of man's essential goodness, and encouraged him toward a greater emphasis on the necessity of grace. *Eighty-Three Different Questions* provides short but valuable glimpses into how his beliefs are evolving. In question 2, he writes, "man is better who is good freely than the man who is good by necessity. Accordingly free will was a fitting and appropriate gift for man."[1] Scott MacDonald says, God created humans with free choice, which makes them "capable of radical initiatives for which they are responsible."[2] This free choice and its corresponding moral responsibility are what distinguish men from animals. In question 24, Augustine claims God would not punish sin or reward right conduct for someone, "who has done nothing of his own will. Accordingly sin and right conduct result from a free choice of the will."[3] As in his early works, reward and punishment demand the will's freedom to make choices between moral alternatives.

Augustine takes a deeper look at Romans 9 and the doctrine of election in question 68. For the first time, he calls fallen mankind a "mass of sin," suggesting, "our nature sinned in paradise."[4] This notion that the whole of human nature sinned in a united way when Adam sinned, is a theme which he will repeat frequently in his later works to support his doctrine of original sin. In question 68, he still believes those in the

---

1. Augustine, *Eighty-Three Questions*, 2.
2. MacDonald, "Primal Sin," 116.
3. Augustine, *Eighty-Three Questions*, 24.
4. Ibid., 68.3.

mass of sin are free to choose to "not be clay" and become the sons of God through believing.[5] He admits God has mercy on whom he wants but insists, "this will of God cannot be unjust."[6] In accord with his early understanding of moral responsibility, he explains, even though sinners constitute a single mass of sin, "it is not the case that there is no difference among them."[7]

Augustine concludes that this difference must be the absence or presence of faith, which is the act of believing he places between *gratia* (grace) and *adiutorium* (divine aid).[8] *Gratia* is consistently presented as being freely offered to all without distinction, while *adiutorium* follows upon the reception of God's offer of grace by a decision of faith.[9] Faith is man's decision to welcome *gratia*, then *adiutorium* is given to aid him to do good works.[10] TeSelle is adamant that the distinction between *gratia* and *adiutorium* is not merely a matter of terminology: "Intervening between these two divine acts of *gratia* and *adiutorium* is the decision of faith, man's own decision to believe the promise of God and to rely upon divine help, forsaking the attempt to gain salvation by himself; and aid is given only to those who respond to the gospel with faith."[11] Augustine believes election is based on something in the human heart, which he calls "deeply hidden merits."[12] God must see something that explains why he has mercy on one and not another, since he would be arbitrary or unjust if there was no difference between them. Faith is the human decision to believe God's offer of grace and receive divine favor.

Augustine teaches that the will is "urged on" by grace, yet also instructs that grace "produces in us even the willing itself."[13] He assumes some of the called refuse to come to God and grace can be rejected without diminishing the quality of the call, yet, at the same time contends, "the calling determines the will."[14] He appears to be struggling to deter-

---

5. Ibid.
6. Ibid., 68.4.
7. Ibid.
8. Ibid., 68.5.
9. TeSelle, *Augustine the Theologian*, 177.
10. Ibid., 162.
11. Ibid.
12. Augustine, *Eighty-Three Questions*, 68.4.
13. Ibid., 68.5.
14. Ibid.

Free to Say No?

mine whether the will that has been called by God is free to say "No" to that call.

In *Propositions from the Epistle to the Romans*, Augustine's view of grace is similar to what we saw in *Eighty-Three Different Questions*. God's call precedes merit and the sinner who follows the call of his own free will receives the Holy Spirit, who helps him to merit eternal life.[15] This call may be freely accepted or rejected, so that election is based on God's foreknowledge of faith.[16] "If he does not choose according to merit, it is not election, for all are equal prior to merit and no choice can be made between absolutely equal things. But since he gives the Holy Spirit only to believers, God indeed does not choose works . . . but rather faith. For unless each one believes in him and perseveres in his willingness to receive, he does not receive the gift of God."[17]

Augustine recognizes fallen man no longer has free will as fully as Adam did, but he does not believe it has been totally destroyed. The fallen will remains capable of desiring good but lacks the power to fulfill this desire. "We do not have free will so as not to sin, but only so much that we do not want to sin. But with grace, not only do we want to act rightly, but we can."[18] Man's free will remains, "whether for belief in God so that mercy follows, or for impiety followed by punishment."[19] Again, we see the principle of alternate possibilities that we observed throughout his early works. Augustine explicitly denies faith comes only from God, stating, "Nowhere is it said, 'God believes all things to all' . . . Belief is our work, but good deeds are his who gives the Holy Spirit."[20] He writes, "It is we who believe and will, but he who gives those believing and willing the ability to do good works through the Holy Spirit."[21] By the free choice of the will, man responds to *gratia* by either assenting or dissenting. If he assents to grace by believing, then he is aided with *adiutorium* so that he may do good works.

---

15. Augustine, *Propositions from Romans*, 60.14–15.
16. Ibid., 60.4.
17. Ibid., 60.71–11.
18. Ibid., 18.12.
19. Ibid., 62.13.
20. Ibid., 60.12.
21. Ibid., 61.7.

In *Retractations*, Augustine attempts to modify some statements he made in *Propositions from the Epistle to the Romans*. He explains, "I had not yet sought diligently enough or discovered up to this time what is the nature of the 'election of grace.'"[22] He replaces his declaration, "It is we who believe and will," with an assertion that the good will and faith are gifts of God.[23] He tries to harmonize these two views by writing, "Both [good will and faith] are ours, then, because of free choice of will, and both, moreover, have been given because of a 'spirit of faith.'"[24] This explanation is confusing considering that by the time he wrote *Retractations*, he no longer believed the assent by which we believe the gospel comes "from ourselves" or is "our very own."[25]

Augustine continues to emphasize that man's will was corrupted by the fall, so that he needs the help of grace to live rightly. This corruption impedes his ability to do the good he desires, but the power to believe remains in the will. William Mann notes Augustine's emphasis was on the "difficulty," but not the impossibility of doing good. He writes, "It is no part of Augustine's message that humans have been *shattered* by the fall."[26] Fallen man remains capable of willing the good, believing in God's grace, and receiving God's help to do good. Carol Harrison summarizes Augustine's position on free will, prior to writing *To Simplician*, "Augustine has qualified his attempt to preserve some element of free will so much that he has arrived at a position in which it is hanging by a very fine thread indeed. The will is only free to choose faith: before it can believe it must be called by God; after it has believed, it can have no effect and can do no good works, without the gift of grace through the Holy Spirit. The will operates freely and alone only in the single moment of faith; a momentary flicker of independent human willing."[27]

J. Patout Burns explains, "Divine mercy provides the situation in which a person can choose to do the good and helps the person to do the good he has chosen; it does not supply the choice itself."[28] That God

---

22. Augustine, *Retractations*, 1.22.2.
23. Ibid., 1.22.3.
24. Ibid.
25. Augustine, *Predestination of the Saints*, 3.7.
26. Mann, "Evil and Original Sin," 47.
27. Harrison, *Rethinking*, 141.
28. Burns, *Operative Grace*, 21.

does not supply the choice itself is a crucial point. There is no causally determined will in Augustine's works before *To Simplician*. "Grace is offered freely to all men," says TeSelle, "its reception in faith is their own act, then the aid of the Holy Spirit is given to them."[29] God offers his mercy, but allows human wills to choose whether or not to accept his grace.

The Donatist controversy may have played an important role in moving Augustine toward the doctrine of efficacious grace, by magnifying the importance of baptism and Catholic Church membership, which were both central issues in his struggles with the Donatists.[30] Having battled to confirm the saving nature of infant baptism, Augustine begins pointing to this rite as an illustration of grace, in his controversy with the Pelagians.[31] Having strongly emphasized the importance of membership in the Catholic Church against the Donatists, he begins adopting a social view of grace that allows him to justify the integration of resistant Donatist believers into the Catholic Church, even by coercion. Brown suggests, Augustine's growing comfort with the use of compulsion in religion may have flowed out of this new understanding of grace. He explains, "His ideas on grace and predestination, for instance, had grown more deeply-rooted in him. He would fall back on them now, to palliate the situation in which he found himself. He had to absorb communities of reluctant Donatists: but he could reassure himself with the belief, that God's grace was able to bring about a change of heart even in men who had been forced into the Catholic Church."[32]

This controversy may have also affected his analysis of how grace operates on individuals.[33] Against the Donatists, he argued that grace does what it needs to do in order to break the custom of sin (Donatism).[34] Burns notes, "Augustine's justification of the use of coercion in religion signals a significant shift in his understanding of freedom. In earlier explanations he limited God's role in human decisions to persuasion and

---

29. TeSelle, *Augustine the Theologian*, 177.
30. Burns, *Development*, 30.
31. Bonner, "Pelagians," 229.
32. Brown, *Augustine of Hippo*, 231.
33. Burns, *Development*, 53.
34. Ibid., 75.

subsequent assistance to those who ask his help. He protected the human person from being forced to act against his desires."[35]

Once he accepted coercion as a loving act toward the Donatists, he eventually deemed it an acceptable practice for the entire church. In one of his sermons, he preaches, "Compel them to come in . . . They are stuck fast in the hedges, and they don't want to be compelled. 'Let us come in of our own free will,' they say. That wasn't the order the Lord gave: 'Compel them,' he said, 'to come in.' Let necessity be experienced outwardly, and hence free willingness to be born inwardly."[36]

Burns believes Augustine's radical doctrine of operative grace did not arise directly out of his study of the Pauline epistles, but rather was formed in the social and ecclesial context of the Donatist controversy.[37]

To Simplician

We have arrived at a crucial moment in Augustine's theological journey. In 396, he wrote a response to two questions from Simplicianus, the bishop in Milan. As his pen touched the parchment, the epicenter of a theological earthquake began rumbling. In *To Simplician*, he dramatically revises his doctrine of election. TeSelle writes, "the reversal of Augustine's understanding of election is not hard to pinpoint, for it occurs between the first and second replies to some questions of Simplicianus."[38] Harrison says, Augustine's thought underwent the most crucial change of his life at this time.[39] Augustine later attests, it was in writing *To Simplician* that he resolved his confusions about election, grace, and faith.[40]

The first question Augustine sought to answer in *To Simplician*, was how to interpret Rom 7:7–25. He suggests the apostle is describing a man under the law and not yet under grace.[41] Paul's statement, "to will is present with me" shows "actual willing is in our power."[42] He goes on to

---

35. Ibid., 77.
36. Augustine, *Sermon 112*, 8.
37. Burns, *Development*, 87.
38. TeSelle, *Augustine the Theologian*, 178.
39. Harrison, *Christian Truth*, 87.
40. Augustine, *Gift of Perseverance*, 20.52.
41. Augustine, *To Simplician*, 1.1.1.
42. Ibid., 1.1.11.

explain, "nothing is easier for a man under the law than to will to do good and yet to do evil. He has no difficulty in willing, but it is not so easy to do what he wills."[43] Difficulty (*difficultas*) affects our power to do good, but does not render us incapable of willing good.[44] Augustine attests, "one thing remains for free will, not that a man may fulfill righteousness when he wishes, but that he may turn with suppliant piety to him who can give the power to fulfill it."[45] This view of free will is similar to what we have seen in his early works.

The majority of *To Simplician* deals with the second question on how to interpret Rom 9:10–29. Augustine instructs that election is not be based on foreknowledge of faith, as he had previously supposed, but must be based on God's own divine purposes. With this in mind, he begins exploring the idea that God can control a person's decisions without violating his free will.[46] An efficacious quality of grace had first been hinted at in *Eighty-Three Different Questions*, but in *To Simplician*, Augustine fully embraces efficacious grace. It is generally accepted that the theological views he would later expound against Pelagius were initially formed into a cohesive theological argument in *To Simplician*.[47]

The important change in Augustine's view of election was his abandoning of faith as the basis for election. Church fathers had almost unanimously taught that election was based on foreknowledge of faith and Augustine had originally followed their lead.[48] Now, he abandons this position, suggesting foreknowledge of faith would not be substantially different from foreknowledge of works. This leads him to reject faith as the basis for election and reevaluate his theories of grace and human willing. He writes, "I do not know how it could be said that it is vain for God to have mercy unless we willingly consent. If God has mercy, we also will, for the power to will is given with the mercy."[49] This is a dramatic departure from his early position insisting the will must be in the power of the will. Now, he appears to be teaching that God causes the willing

---

43. Ibid., 1.1.12.
44. Wetzel, "*Simplicianum, Ad*," 798.
45. Augustine, *To Simplician*, 1.1.14.
46. Burns, *Development*, 37.
47. Harrison, *Rethinking*, 6.
48. Schaff, *History of the Christian Church*, 852.
49. Augustine, *To Simplician*, 1.2.12.

itself, making a person will what God wants. The will's consent inevitably follows God's offer of mercy, rather than being the condition upon which mercy is received. According to TeSelle, Augustine, "is now persuaded that election to grace (or refusal of mercy) comes prior to any decision on man's part. Whether a man believes or does not is decided by God."[50]

In examining *To Simplician*, we find three primary concerns that drove Augustine to alter his doctrine of election. His first concern is the fear that accepting foreknown faith as the basis for election, would obligate him to accept foreknown works as an equally valid basis for election. "If election is by foreknowledge, and God foreknew Jacob's faith," he asks, "how do you prove that he did not elect him for his works?"[51] If election is based on something God foresees in man, then what distinguishes foreseen faith from foreseen works? His opponents argue faith is distinguished from works in Romans 4:5, so faith may rightly serve as the basis for election. However, Augustine is convinced that merit accrues from willing, so election based on faith would be merited. He concludes that faith cannot be the basis for election any more than works can.

Augustine is uncomfortable with his conclusion because it makes election appear arbitrary. He wrestled with this issue in *Eighty-Three Different Questions*, when he quickly retreated from the doctrine of unconditional election because he felt it would raise questions about God's justice.[52] In *To Simplician*, he commits himself to unconditional election, though he is still unsure how it can be just or how there can be any election at all if there is no difference between Jacob and Esau. He attempts to resolve this dilemma by suggesting God creates the distinction between them. Jacob is not chosen because he is good, but he is made good by God, so that he might be chosen.[53] This does nothing to resolve the issue of arbitrariness though, since God still has to choose which persons to make good. The choice is still arbitrary if there is no difference to explain why one is chosen and not another. Nonetheless, Augustine remains convinced Romans 9 teaches that God can elect whomever he wants, and he searches for ways to explain how this is just. Wetzel says, "In *Ad Simplicianum*, Augustine is concerned to disencumber God's sovereignty over the

---

50. TeSelle, *Augustine the Theologian*, 178.
51. Augustine, *To Simplician*, 1.2.5.
52. Augustine, *Eighty-Three Questions*, 68.6.
53. Augustine, *To Simplician*, 1.2.4.

work of redemption from constraints of any stripe."[54] To do this he "handily" disposes of both juridical and volitional constraints, by appealing to divine omnipotence.[55] Because God is the all-powerful ruler, he can save whomever he chooses and does not need human consent to do so.

Augustine's second concern revolves around Paul's assertion that election took place, "when they were not yet born." He took this to mean nothing Esau or Jacob did on earth could have differentiated them for election, because election took place prior to their births. When he looks for justification of God's rejection of Esau, by suggesting Esau may have lacked faith, he quickly concludes this cannot be the explanation. "Neither Jacob nor Esau had yet believed," he explains, "because they were not yet born and had done neither good nor evil."[56] If God's foreknowledge of their lives had no influence on his choice, then neither their faith nor their unbelief can be the basis for election. The only thing left, according to Augustine, was God's hidden purpose.[57]

Augustine's third concern is his belief that the primary message of Romans 9 was, "that no man should glory in meritorious works, in which the Israelites dared to glory, alleging that they had served the law that had been given them, and for that reason they had received evangelical grace as due to their merits."[58] He believes this theme dominates the whole Epistle of Romans. With this in mind, he interprets the phrases, "so it does not depend on the man who wills" and "so that God's purpose according to election would stand, not because of works but because of Him who calls," to be guideposts which show the basis for election rests solely on the purposes of God and not on foreknowledge of man's will.[59]

Having proposed the doctrine of unconditional election, Augustine never retreated and during his battles with the Pelagians he became more entrenched than ever. He still had some concerns about his new position and passionately expressed one major doubt over and over again in *To Simplician*, "What do we say about Esau?"[60] He calls this a "knotty

---

54. Wetzel, "Pelagius Anticipated," 124.
55. Ibid., 140.
56. Augustine, *To Simplician*, 1.2.4.
57. Ibid., 1.2.6.
58. Ibid., 1.2.2.
59. Ibid., 1.2.6.
60. Ibid., 1.2.8.

Augustine's Middle Works

problem" and frequently returns to it to try to resolve it. "If Esau was rejected for no fault of his own," he asks, "How can his rejection be said to be just?"[61] "How did Esau deserve to be hated before he was born? That God made one he was to love is unquestionably true. But it is absurd to say that he made someone he was going to hate."[62] He wonders, "Why was Esau not shown mercy?"[63]

Augustine recognizes the unmerited nature of Jacob's election implies that Esau's rejection must also be unmerited, since he had done nothing good or evil when he was rejected.[64] It is clear that if he claims Esau was rejected because of his foreknown evil deeds, he would also have to admit Jacob was chosen for his foreknown good deeds. He doubts God's hatred of Esau can be just if it was unmerited, yet quickly recoils from this thought, writing, "If we admit this, then Jacob must be loved because he had merited to be loved by his justice. And if that is true, it is false to say that it was not of works."[65]

Augustine labors to find a reason for Esau's rejection. He again considers unbelief but reasons that if Jacob was chosen without foreknowledge of his faith, then Esau must have been rejected without consideration of his foreknown unbelief.[66] Finally, finding no good answer for why Esau was rejected, he exhorts his readers, "Let us believe that this belongs to a certain hidden equity that cannot be searched out by any human standard of measurement."[67] Wetzel judges this claim of "hidden equity" to be contradictory to the doctrine of unconditional election. Election cannot be gratuitous and still be based on some hidden difference. He claims, "Augustine is willing to tolerate this contradiction in order to preserve the appearance of God's justice."[68] Augustine further suggests God "decides who are not to be offered mercy by a standard of equity which is most secret and far removed from human powers of understanding."[69] He assures

---

61. Ibid., 1.2.4.
62. Ibid., 1.2.8.
63. Ibid.1.2.10.
64. Ibid., 1.2.8.
65. Ibid.
66. Ibid., 1.2.10.
67. Ibid., 1.2.16.
68. Wetzel, "Predestination," 53.
69. Augustine, *To Simplician*, 1.2.16.

us, "God does not hate Esau the man, but hates Esau the sinner."[70] Yet, according to his own argument, God's hatred of Esau preceded his birth and was not based on his personal sins. This inconsistency will eventually lead him to determine that God hates the reprobate for the sin they committed together in Adam's loins.

TeSelle says, Augustine assumed original sin "was sufficient cause for damnation, without any personal sins being added."[71] This is evident from his insistence the reprobate are "rejected for no fault of their own."[72] They are not rejected for their sins or their unbelief. There is no reason in them for why they are rejected, "hated,"[73] or why mercy is "withheld."[74] Election is based solely on God's mysterious choice. Yet, Augustine continues to inquire, "Why was this mercy withheld from Esau?"[75] And again, "Why did his mercy fail in Esau's case?"[76] He considers the rejection of the reprobate a "divine penalty, as if God abandons a man by not calling him in a way in which he might be moved by faith."[77] Yet, in the end, we have no valid explanation for why he is abandoned. We have only the assertion that God's hatred, rejection, and abandonment of the reprobate was not based on their own personal sins or unbelief, but solely on some hidden purpose of God. Wetzel remarks, "The issue of reprobation has always been the bane of scholarship on Augustine . . . The problem for Augustine's apologists has been that there is no accounting for divine judgment other than by the unhappy device of original sin. This is to explain the obscure by the more obscure."[78]

To explain how those who obtain mercy actually come to faith, Augustine offers a long description of how God "calls" people in an "effectual" way, which always produces its intended results.[79] Having rejected any distinction between human wills, he proposes a distinction in the way God calls people. God calls some in a way that fails to cause faith, while

70. Ibid., 1.2.18.
71. TeSelle, *Augustine the Theologian*, 323.
72. Augustine, *To Simplician*, 1.2.4.
73. Ibid., 1.2.8.
74. Ibid.
75. Ibid., 1.2.9.
76. Ibid., 1.2.10.
77. Ibid., 1.2.14.
78. Wetzel, *Virtue*, 207–8.
79. Augustine, *To Simplician*, 1.2.13–14.

he calls others in a way that causes the will's consent to faith.[80] The call itself, "is the effectual cause of the good will so that everyone who is called follows it."[81] He continues, "For the effectiveness of God's mercy cannot be in the power of man to frustrate, if he will have none of it. If God wills to have mercy on men, he can call them in a way that is suited to them, so that they will be moved to understand and to follow . . . Those who are chosen are effectually (*congruenter*) called . . . He calls the man on whom he has mercy in the way he knows will suit him, so that he will not refuse the call."[82]

While Augustine says, the effectual call is the "cause" of the good will, he does not yet relinquish some role for the will. The reason for the call's effectiveness is that it is suits the desires of the one being called. The Latin word, *congruenter*, means the call is congruent or suited to the will, so that the will finds it attractive and responds positively to it. Augustine urges, God could have even called Esau in an effectual or congruent way, if he had so desired.[83] TeSelle says Augustine's teaching that faith depends on the call of grace was not new. What was new was the claim that this call "is not issued to all with the same force, and whether or not a man believes is dependent on the character of the call."[84] Augustine's reversal on the doctrine of election is now forcing changes in his understanding of God's call and grace.

In *Free Will*, Augustine wrote that the will must be attracted by something it perceives, but the will remained free to decide how to react to these perceptions.[85] This left the free choice of the will as the deciding factor in whether a person would respond to God's call positively or negatively. Scott believes Augustine has begun discarding this view because he cannot endorse the notion that an eternal, immutable, omnipotent God reacts to humans in any way.[86] In *To Simplician*, God's call is the deciding factor in the will's response, not man's free choice.

---

80. Ibid., 1.2.12.
81. Ibid., 1.2.13.
82. Ibid.
83. Ibid., 1.2.14.
84. TeSelle, *Augustine the Theologian*, 179.
85. Augustine, *Free Will*, 2.25.74.
86. Scott, *Augustine*, 180.

Free to Say No?

At times in *To Simplician*, Augustine seems to be suggesting God attracts the affections of the will by external motivations or interior wooing but allows the will to maintain freedom to say "No" to his wooing. The elect, he says, are those who "have not despised him who calls, but have believed and followed him." The congruent call appears to allow the possibility of dissent, but the call is so attractive that the will freely chooses to assent to it. Yet, in the same paragraph Augustine asserts, "what we actually will he [God] alone gives."[87] When he writes, "He [God] freely bestows on us voluntary assent,"[88] he is presenting a unilateral action of God that appears stronger than just a congruent invitation. TeSelle observes that in Augustine's early works, the will did not control the "suasions" it perceived, but "consenting or not consenting to these suasions is the act of the will itself."[89] His new contention that God alone gives or causes the will, according to Harrison, is a "final, irrevocable step" toward attributing man's will and faith "wholly to the action of God's grace."[90] Basil Studer agrees, "the divine will is seen as absolutely sovereign while human freedom is seriously called in question."[91] Augustine is committing himself to a grace which is effectual, not just congruent, because it actually causes good human willing, including the assent of the will. If man cannot frustrate God's will to have mercy on him, then choosing between assent and dissent is no longer an option for the will. TeSelle suggests that from this point onward, when Augustine uses "assent" or "consent" language, he "does not mean to suggest that man's consenting or not consenting to the divine call is determined by his own decision."[92] He writes, "Therefore, when he says that the consenting or not consenting is man's own, he cannot mean that man himself decides the issue with what the scholastics would call 'freedom of exercise,' the freedom to act or not to act, for the act of the will is evoked by the persuasive quality of the call."[93]

---

87. Augustine, *To Simplician*, 1.2.10.
88. Ibid., 1.2.21.
89. TeSelle, *Augustine the Theologian*, 287.
90. Harrison, *Truth*, 88.
91. Studer, *The Grace of Christ*, 103.
92. TeSelle, *Augustine the Theologian*. 287.
93. Ibid.

Augustine's Middle Works

His theory of the congruent call for the elect demands as its corollary some explanation for the fate of the reprobate. If God is able to call anyone in a congruent way, including Esau, "Why was this mercy withheld from Esau?"[94] Why is it withheld from the majority of God's creation? TeSelle states, God's decision to not call the reprobate in an effectual way is derived from "nothing else than his deciding not to have mercy on them."[95] That God withholds mercy from so many is not based on their sins, unbelief, or rejection of his call. According to Augustine, God's refusal of mercy is based solely on his own pleasure and will. Studer resolves, "Augustine undoubtedly limits the saving will of God" to a select few.[96]

Before *To Simplician*, Augustine had said that man's decision of faith stood between *gratia* and *adiutorium* and was man's own decision.[97] Now, he says the presence of *gratia* insures faith will be the decision of the will. Harrison reasons, "It is grace, and only grace, which liberates the will and enables it to will the good. This is what is explicitly taught in the closing chapters of the *Ad Simplicianum* in 396."[98] As to why God does not call all sinners congruently, Augustine can only vouch that the reprobate are never passed over unjustly. Their condemnation is just, based on their guilt for Adam's sin.[99]

To support this view of original guilt, Augustine reintroduces the concept of *massa peccati*, which lumps all of mankind together as a single mass of sin—permeated with the guilt of Adam's sin. He claims the original sin of Adam makes "the entire human race" sinful and deserving of condemnation.[100] John Burnaby believes Augustine's *massa peccati* theory, "*prima facie* is irreconcilable with belief in God's justice."[101] Adam's descendants are held guilty for a sin they did not participate in willingly. Bavinck says, "According to Augustine, only original sin logically precedes predestination. Moreover, he considers original sin to be a

---

94. Augustine, *To Simplician*, 1.2.10.
95. TeSelle, *Augustine the Theologian*, 179.
96. Studer, *The Grace of Christ*, 102.
97. Augustine, *Eighty-Three Questions*, 68.3.
98. Harrison, *Rethinking*, 99.
99. Wetzel, *Virtue*, 155–6.
100. Augustine, *To Simplician*, 1.2.16.
101. Burnaby, *Amor*, 196.

sufficient ground for reprobation. Actual sins are not taken into account in the decree of reprobation."[102]

Augustine's opponents argue that the damnation of Adam's descendants for a sin they did not commit cannot be considered just by any standard. Augustine's appeal to mystery is insufficient, since our basic moral idea of justice must in some way be based upon God's justice.[103] If we are "unable to grasp divine justice," Rist asserts, "we can hardly know anything about human justice either."[104] If God's justice is so different from human justice that we cannot begin to understand it, then it would be irrational for God to command us to act justly. In his later works, Augustine, himself, will admit he struggles to understand how this doctrine can be just if souls are created by God.[105]

Augustine's assertion that grace causes "voluntary assent" is another troubling proposition for many scholars. Wetzel asks, "Can consent be both voluntary and caused? For Augustine the conjunction must hold. If consent is not voluntary, it is not consent. If consent is not caused, God does not have control over the calling."[106] This redefining of "voluntary" is inconsistent with the definition from his early works, where consent which is natural, necessary, or compelled is not "voluntary." Augustine now calls the caused will, "voluntary," but his doctrine of grace is steadily eviscerating its voluntary nature.

Before leaving *To Simplician*, we must note one final development that begins to surface in this book. Wetzel observes that Augustine now believes, "no one has a desire for God—not a scintilla of it—who has not been predestined by God to have it. In stark contrast, desire that originates with human beings is always dark."[107] Augustine has steadily weakened the will's power until it is no longer capable of moving the soul toward any good desire or action. Grace alone moves the soul toward good.[108] This continual darkening of the human condition and the eviscerating of the power of the will become dominant themes in his anti-Pelagian writings.

---

102. Bavinck, "The Doctrine of God," 1.
103. Burns, *Development*, 198–9.
104. Rist, "Free Will and Predestination," 440.
105. Augustine, *Letter 166*, 10.1.
106. Wetzel, *Virtue*, 157.
107. Wetzel, "Predestination," 157.
108. Riches, "Readings of Augustine," 185.

Augustine's Middle Works

Confessions to Punishment and Forgiveness of Sins

Around 398, Augustine finished *Confessions*, which intermingles his personal testimony with his developing theory of grace. In this book, his wandering soul finds its way home through many years of searching and some illuminating moments of grace. Grace is constantly wooing and calling him home, but his will also plays a role in this drama, both resisting and responding to grace. Augustine confesses to being a sinner who is at times, totally closed to God's wooing;[109] at other times, open to it, though delaying his response;[110] and at still other times, passionately ready to respond to the call of his divine lover.[111]

The structure of *Confessions* is similar to the story of the prodigal son. Augustine grows up in a house of faith, but wanders into the world because of his own lust and pride. Eventually, he sinks into the pit of Manichaeism and vanity. There, he is reminded of home by the writings of the Neo-Platonists. At one point they help him experience a beautiful vision, where he sees his divine father. He follows the path they show him, ignoring temporal things and seeking only to find the eternal. Upon arriving home, he discovers his father has been watching his progress, even planting signposts along the way to guide him home. He knows that without his father's help he would never have made it home, so he praises him for his grace. While this is an extremely paraphrased version of *Confessions*, it represents the way God's grace worked both in and with Augustine's will to bring him to the saving knowledge of Jesus Christ.

In chapter 7 of *Confessions*, Augustine writes, "But one thing lifted me up toward thy light: it was that I had come to know that I had a will as certainly as I knew that I had a life. When, therefore, I willed or was unwilling to do something, I was utterly certain that it was none but myself who willed or was unwilling — and immediately I realized that there was the cause of my sin."[112]

He is proposing "the presence of a mediating faculty, the will, which could determine itself in accord with either rational or irrational desires while retaining its independence from both."[113] This is a crucial proposi-

---

109. Augustine, *Confessions*, 3.3.5.
110. Ibid., 6.4.6.
111. Ibid., 3.4.8.
112. Ibid., 7.3.5.
113. Wetzel, *Virtue*, 3.

tion because this notion of the will requires that choice have a measure of independence from desire or we are left with nothing but habitual action. Lust came from his will, but only when he had yielded to it repeatedly did it become habit. Then, "habit, not resisted, became necessity."[114] His will was not enslaved to sinful desires at birth, but became enslaved to these desires by habitually yielding to them. This is very similar to the way he presented the will in the *Debate with Fortunatus*.

In book 9, Augustine asks the important question, "Where during all those years was my free will"?[115] TeSelle answers, "His will was there, but it was immobilized by internal conflict."[116] "Why, therefore, do I delay in abandoning my hopes of this world," wonders Augustine, "and giving myself wholly to seek after God and the blessed life?"[117] Grace was at work in his life, but his will remained free to either submit to it or resist it. He laments, "Thus my two wills—the old and the new, the carnal and the spiritual—were in conflict within me; and by their discord they tore my soul apart."[118]

Augustine rejected the Manichean belief that within the soul there was a battle between two natures. Instead, he posits a battle between two wills. His old will desires temporal things, while a new will, rising within him with the help of grace, desires eternal things. This struggle leads to a state of "volitional paralysis."[119] In book 10, he says, "I neither willed entirely, nor was entirely unwilling."[120] In book 11, he writes, "I said mentally, 'Lo let it be done now, let it be done now.' And as I spoke, I all but came to a resolve. I all but did it, yet I did it not . . . And I tried again . . . and yet came not at it."[121] Babcock calls this divided will, "a struggle between competing desires within a single self."[122] Grace is at work in Augustine's life, but his old will is resisting. He still loves temporal things, even though he has come to love eternal things too. He is being drawn

---

114. Augustine, *Confessions*, 8.5.10.
115. Ibid., 9.1.1.
116. TeSelle, *Augustine the Theologian*, 42.
117. Augustine, *Confessions*, 6.10.19.
118. Ibid., 8.5.10.
119. Wetzel, *Virtue*, 135.
120. Augustine, *Confessions*, 10.22.
121. Ibid., 11.25.
122. Babcock, "Spirituality of Desire," 180.

in both directions, but it is his will alone which is left to make the choice between these two competing desires.

Augustine's divided will is puzzling to some, because the will in *To Simplician* appears to be ruled by one desire or another. Some scholars ask where the conflict comes from if the effectual call causes the will to delight in good. TeSelle believes Augustine's theory of willing still requires that sin or conversion be a free act of the will, which is "genuinely the act of the creatures themselves."[123] The will freely chooses between competing desires and is therefore morally responsible for its choice.

Brachtendorf says the power of the old will is finally broken in *Confessions* by the "helping hand" model of grace, which was first presented in *Free Will*. In this "helping hand" model, God offers grace to all. He empowers the new will to overcome the old will, when a person assents to his help. The will is the mechanism of choice between the new will and the old will. Grace helps the will to choose good, but does not obligate this choice. Wetzel states, "Augustine worked through the notion of will as choice before finding it unserviceable and moving on to a far more complex understanding."[124] However, in *Confessions*, as in many of the middle works, the will remains free to choose how it will respond to grace.

In *Answer to Felix*, written about eight years after *To Simplician*, the will remains free to choose its own disposition. Augustine quotes Matt 12:33, "Either make the tree good, or make the tree bad," then offers the interpretation, "When, therefore, he says, 'Either do this or do that,' he indicates a power . . . each person has it in his will either to choose what is good and to be a good tree or to choose what is evil and to be a bad tree."[125] Augustine's interpretation is crucial because it affirms the power of the will to choose whether to be a good will or an evil will. Since Jesus is addressing fallen men, this power of choice must be present in fallen man and not just in Adam. Augustine states, "if they chose the good, they would receive a reward from him, while if they chose evil, they would feel punishment from him."[126] The choice between alternate possibilities appears evident in this interpretation.

---

123. TeSelle, *Augustine the Theologian*, 202.
124. Wetzel, *Virtue*, 7.
125. Augustine, *Answer to Felix*, 2.4.
126. Ibid., 2.5.

Free to Say No?

Augustine says "free choice" means, "One who is unwilling to observe the law has it in his power to do so, if he wills . . . For, if they are forced, they are not unwilling but are unable."[127] He adds, "What lies, then, in their own will—namely, that they are unwilling to observe the law—is a sin without any compulsion."[128] He concludes, "from this you will see the source from which all sins come, from which all meriting of punishment comes, and from which all assigning of punishment comes."[129] As in his early works, Augustine insists moral responsibility comes from the power to say "No" and guilt demands the absence of compulsion.

When Felix asks why some sinners are not purified, Augustine answers, "Because they did not want to be." Felix asks, "Did you say, 'Because they did not want to be?'" Augustine replies, "I said, 'Because they did not want to be.' It is evident that our will is in our power and I have proved this from the divine Scriptures."[130] In this debate, his doctrines of unconditional election and effectual grace are taking a back seat to his commitment to free will and moral responsibility. Man's eternal destiny rests in the power of his will, which has the power to say "Yes" or "No" to both sin and grace.

Despite continuing to defend his early view of moral responsibility, Augustine keeps developing his doctrine of original sin in other works written around this time. In *Ten Homilies on the First Epistle of St. John*, he says all men are judged sinners worthy of condemnation because of their birth as sons of Adam.[131] In *Letter 98*, he writes that each infant contracts sin "because it was one with Adam and in Adam from whom the child contracted it when the sin that was contracted was committed."[132] TeSelle believes the doctrine of original sin was the key difference between Augustine and Pelagius, who would never accept Augustine's claim that original sin by itself, without any personal sins, was sufficient for the damnation of infants.[133]

---

127. Ibid.
128. Ibid.
129. Ibid.
130. Ibid., 2.12.
131. Augustine, *Ten Homilies*, 4.11.
132. Augustine, *Letter 98*, 1.
133. TeSelle, *Augustine the Theologian*, 283.

Augustine's Middle Works

In *Retractations*, Augustine explains that *Punishment and Forgiveness of Sins*, written around 411, "focused principally on the baptism of little ones on account of original sin."[134] Infant baptism and original sin may appear unrelated to the doctrines of election, grace and will, but Augustine's fervor to win the point on them reveals how important he considered them to be for supporting his evolved positions. Original sin explains God's decision to condemn the reprobate before they ever sinned. it validates their being punished with a nature that sins necessarily. Infant baptism supports his notions of effectual grace and human willing. If infants are condemned by original sin at birth and redeemed by grace at baptism, without ever using their wills in either sin or redemption, then the assent or dissent of the will is irrelevant to one's election.

Augustine insists original sin was passed on to Adam's descendants "by propagation, not by imitation."[135] That is, all men became sinners by their birth and not by their decision to imitate Adam and sin. He quotes Rom 5:12, a text that in his Old Latin translation said, "in whom all have sinned,"[136] and concludes that all Adam's descendants actually sinned "in Adam."[137] Gerald Bonner does not believe the original Greek text supports Augustine's translation, since the text is properly translated "inasmuch as all sinned."[138] Some scholars admit Augustine's translation of Rom 5:12 is flawed, yet argue that his interpretation might still give the proper sense of the whole chapter.[139] Whether or not we accept the validity of this interpretation of Rom 5:12, it is clearly inconsistent with the principles of moral responsibility Augustine established in his early works, which required participation of the will for an action to be considered sin.

Even as he condemns infants for Adam's sin, Augustine maintains that these infants "have committed nothing evil by means of their own will, without which there can be no sin belonging to one's own life."[140] He calls them "innocent" and declares that their inabilities and weaknesses at birth "demonstrate their freedom from personal sin with a silence that

---

134. Augustine, *Retractations*, 2.33.60.
135. Augustine, *Punishment and Forgiveness*, 1.9.10.
136. Ibid., 1.10.11.
137. Ibid., 1.13.16.
138. Bonner, *Life and Controversies*, 372.
139. Bonner, "They Speak to Us," 237–38.
140. Augustine, *Punishment and Forgiveness*, 1.35.65.

bears stronger witness than any language of ours."[141] He rejects the theory that souls may have sinned in heaven prior to taking on flesh,[142] so we might expect him to deny their participation in Adam's sin prior to birth. This is not the case. He is adamant that infants cannot be guiltless for two reasons. First, there would be no need for them to be forgiven of sins at their baptism unless they were guilty of sin.[143] Second, it would not be just for souls to suffer the weakness and torments of the flesh that infants do, if they were pure from contamination of sin.[144] He suggests infants might have been born with the ability to speak, walk, and run like adults, if the fall had not happened.[145] For these two reasons, he is convinced all infants contract original sin from Adam and are therefore guilty of his sin at their birth.[146]

Augustine cannot explain how original sin is transmitted to infants. He says flesh became sinful in Adam, then this sin was transferred to all so that "only sinful flesh has been begotten," except for Jesus.[147] He wonders if the soul is not propagated in the same way as the flesh, which would be an espousal of the Traducian error.[148] Pelagius defended the creationist view, which argued that Adam's sin cannot be transmitted to his descendants if each soul is created by God and does not come from propagation.[149] Admitting this is a "very obscure matter," Augustine avoids committing himself to any particular method of sin's transmission.[150] Henri Blocher believes Augustine's vacillating explanations are attempts to "sweep under the carpet" the difficulty he has explaining the move from seminal participation in sin to individual responsibility.[151]

Augustine's commitment to original sin appears to be based largely on the practice of infant baptism. If baptism saves infants from sin, they

---

141. Ibid.
142. Ibid., 1.22.31.
143. Ibid., 1.35.66.
144. Ibid., 3.10.18.
145. Ibid., 1.37.68–69.
146. Ibid., 1.13.16.
147. Ibid., 2.36.58.
148. Ibid., 2.36.59.
149. Ibid., 3.3.5.
150. Ibid., 2.36.59.
151. Blocher, *Original Sin*, 115.

must have been guilty of sin at birth.[152] Yet, he also asserts that infants are not forgiven of their own sins, "but for those of another."[153] In his early works, he had insisted that one cannot be condemned by the sins of another, unless he participated in the sin by the exercise of his own will. He also argued that no nature could be corrupted by the fault of another. Now, in a complete reversal, he accepts Cyprian's claim that "the sins of others" are forgiven in infant baptism.[154] Being morally responsible for another's sin is a clear contradiction to his early teaching on sin and moral responsibility.

Augustine tries once more to explain his difficult view, "And these sins are not called those of another, as if they did not belong to the little ones. For they all sinned then in Adam, when they were all still that one man in virtue of that power implanted in his nature by which he was able to beget them. They are, rather, called the sins of another, because the little ones themselves were not yet living their own lives."[155] The inconsistency seems evident. Adam's descendants actually sin in Adam, before they have their own lives. Yet it is not their sin, but the sin of another.

Augustine seems to envision all souls springing forth out of the one soul of Adam. Rist notes how similar this concept is to Plotinus's hypostasis of Soul.[156] Rowan Greer contends, "Augustine's conclusion that we all sinned in Adam's fall represents both a transformation of the older view he inherited and a radical novelty."[157] His theory is at odds with previous church fathers and is at odds with the definition of sin he established in his early works—that sin must be an act of the will. If his early definition of sin applies only to the first sin, as Augustine has begun proposing, it will still fail to be true, since Adam's descendants are guilty for this first sin, though their wills did not participate in any way. If we bear the penalty for the first sin, when we have not sinned "knowingly and with free will," judges Babcock, "the whole scheme of sin and penalty now seems to founder on this point."[158] Indeed, if sin is transferred as Augustine sug-

---

152. Augustine, *Punishment and Forgiveness*, 3.4.7.
153. Ibid., 3.5.10.
154. Ibid.
155. Ibid., 3.7.14.
156. Rist, *Ancient*, 126.
157. Greer, "Sinned We All," 394.
158. Babcock, "Responsibility," 229.

gests, through propagation before there is any involvement of the will, then it would be logical to presume every person would be morally responsible for every sin committed by each of their ancestors.

Despite these inconsistencies, Augustine clung to the doctrine of original sin as the only explanation for the Catholic practice of infant baptism. He believed he found support for this theory in the writings of Cyprian, Tertullian, Ambrose, and Jerome.[159] Numerous Greek fathers had taught that the fall damaged human nature, though they did not teach that it removed all capacity to will the good.[160] Ambrose saw a solidarity with Adam, but taught, "while the corrupting force of sin is transmitted, the guilt attaches to Adam himself, not to us."[161] Ambrosiaster said we are not punished for Adam's sins, but only for our own.[162] In fact, before Augustine, almost all the church fathers stopped short of attributing guilt to Adam's descendants, since guilt was only conceivable where there was a morally responsible agent involved.[163]

Burnaby believes Augustine was never able to adequately explain how this transfer of guilt and moral responsibility can be just. "The only possible answer," says Burnaby, "seemed to be that we bear the 'guilt' of a sin which we have not ourselves committed: the 'innocent' child is at the same time 'guilty.' But then guilt ceases to be ethically intelligible."[164] Either, Adam's descendants are guilty of sinning "in him," without their own wills, or they are guilty for Adam's act of sin. Augustine's early theory of moral responsibility will have to be abandoned in either case.

Augustine contends that the position of the Pelagians was even less tenable than his own, considering the actual form of baptism practiced in the Catholic Church. The sponsor would renounce the devil on behalf of the infant, then say the infant was converted to God and forgiven of his sins. Pelagians denied the infant needed to be converted to God or forgiven of sins.[165] He dismisses their assertion that we only become sinners by imitating Adam's sin, claiming their teachings did not adequately

---

159. Rees, *Pelagius*, 65.
160. Chadwick, *John Cassian*, 123.
161. Kelly, *Early Christian Doctrines*, 354.
162. Ibid., 355.
163. Wiles, *The Christian Fathers*, 98.
164. Burnaby, *Amor*, 191.
165. Augustine, *Punishment and Forgiveness*, 1.34.63.

address Rom 5:18–19. He believes his doctrine of original sin is the only alternative to Pelagianism and the only explanation for infant baptism.

Why were original sin and infant baptism so important to Augustine? The answer is found in *Punishment and Forgiveness of Sins*, when he moves directly from his presentation of original sin and infant baptism to a study of the election of Jacob and Esau in Romans 9.[166] The logic was clear to him. If all men are condemned for Adam's sin and infants are forgiven this sin in baptism, then the will is irrelevant in condemnation and in salvation and election must be unconditional. TeSelle claims infant baptism served as Augustine's ultimate example to confirm his doctrines of grace and predestination.[167] His belief that infants were baptized "for the remission of sins" had been central to his dispute with the Donatists.[168] Now, he concludes that the saving nature of infant baptism proves the gratuitous nature of grace, since infants have neither faith nor works.[169] Faith must be the product of God's grace and not the condition upon which it is received. To Augustine, the package is now a neatly wrapped theological system.

In book 2 of *Punishment and Forgiveness of Sins*, Augustine attempts to harmonize his previous teaching on free will with his evolved views of grace and election. He writes, "God helps those who turn to him, but abandons those who turn away. But he also helps us to turn to him."[170] "After all," he adds, "God is said to be our helper, and we cannot be helped unless we try to do something ourselves, because God does not produce our salvation in us as if we were mindless rocks."[171] He wishes to maintain his commitment to free will, but his conviction that good comes only from God, leads him to resolve, "we must admit that we obtain a good will from God."[172] He is striving for balance, so as "not to defend grace in such a way that we seem to destroy free choice and not to stress free choice in such a way that we are judged ungrateful to the grace of God."[173]

---

166. Ibid., 1.22.31.
167. TeSelle, *Augustine the Theologian*, 322.
168. Rist, *Ancient*, 125.
169. Pelikan, *The Christian Tradition*, 302.
170. Augustine, *Punishment and Forgiveness*, 2.5.5.
171. Ibid., 2.5.6.
172. Ibid., 2.18.30.
173. Ibid., 2.18.28.

This balance, however, is steadily shifting away from free choice of the will and toward the causally determined will and efficacious grace.

Spirit and the Letter

Spirit and the Letter was one of the most important books in the Protestant Reformation. James O'Donnell calls it, "Augustine's most compact and readable exposition of his theology of grace."[174] In this work Augustine objects to the Pelagian view "that the power of the human will can by itself, without the help of God, either attain righteousness or make progress in tending toward it."[175] He insists human beings must be "helped to achieve righteousness" by the Holy Spirit, "so that there arises in their minds a delight in and a love for . . . God."[176] Free choice alone avails for nothing, unless our will "is helped and raised up through the gift of the Spirit of grace."[177] It is through the Spirit's gift that we begin to "delight in not sinning,"[178] and it is grace that renews us in the image of God and heals our wounded souls.[179] Yet, Augustine maintains a limited role for human willing.

> Are we then doing away with free choice through grace? Heaven forbid! Rather we make free choice stronger. After all, as the law is not done away with through faith, so free choice is not done away with, but strengthened by grace. For the law is not fulfilled without free choice. But *knowledge of sin came through the law* (Rom 3:20); through faith we obtain grace to struggle against sin; through the good health of the soul comes freedom of choice; through free choice we have the love of righteousness; through the love of righteousness we fulfill the law.[180]

This is Augustine's "Golden Chain," where he regards free choice as an inalienable right that has lost its strength to choose good. "If then they

---

174. O'Donnell, *Times and Lives*, 5.
175. Augustine, *Spirit and the Letter*, 3.4.
176. Ibid., 3.5.
177. Ibid., 12.20.
178. Ibid., 16.28.
179. Ibid., 27.47.
180. Ibid., 30.52.

are slaves of sin, why do they boast of free choice?"[181] Yet, twice in this section, Augustine also says, faith "obtains" grace. He says, faith "seems to be the beginning of salvation or of this chain leading to salvation."[182] Thus, human belief or unbelief continues to play an essential role in one's salvation.

The key question he proposes is, "whether faith itself... lies in our power?"[183] Understanding Augustine's answer to this question is essential to understanding his theology of grace in *Spirit and the Letter*. He begins his answer by defining the word "power" as "being able" to do something.[184] He notes the distinction between "power" (*potestas*) and will (*voluntas*). Will is that which we will to do and power is that which we are able to do. We cannot always do what we will to do and we do not always will to do what we have the power to do.[185] Having established these definitions, he restates the question, "We are asking whether that faith by which we believe God or believe in God is in our power."[186] It is absurd to believe otherwise, he says, "After all, what is it to believe but to assent that what is said is true? Assent is certainly an act of someone who wills. Hence, faith is surely in our power."[187] Over and over again in his previous works, Augustine has asserted, "the will is in our power." Now, he affirms emphatically that faith is also in our power, because it is an act of will.

There is no contradiction, he instructs, between this view and his emphasis on 1 Cor 4:7, since, "That we believe is God's gift."[188] The Bible says all power comes from God, but it does not say all will comes from God. "Otherwise, if there were no will except from God, God would be—heaven forbid!—the author even of sins."[189] God does not give the evil will, though he does give the power to carry out an evil will, yet, "when power is given, necessity is certainly not imposed."[190] Evil persons "re-

---

181. Ibid.
182. Ibid., 31.53.
183. Ibid.
184. Ibid.
185. Ibid..
186. Ibid., 31.54.
187. Ibid.
188. Ibid.
189. Ibid.
190. Ibid.

ceive power" to demonstrate their evil will, while good persons "receive power for the purpose of proving their good will."[191] He, then, repeats his crucial answer, "Faith, then, is in our power, because we believe when we will, and when we believe, we believe willingly."[192]

Having determined that faith is in our power because it is an act of will, he moves the issue back one step to explore, "whether the will by which we believe is itself a gift of God or arises from the free choice belonging to our nature."[193] He has just argued that all will is not from God, but he does not want to say the good will, or the will to believe is not from God, or humans will have something good that they did not receive from God. Yet, if he says the will to believe is "only the gift of God," then infidels would have an excuse for their unbelief, "because God refused to give them this will."[194] This leads him to a second question, "Why does everyone not have it [the will to believe]?"[195]

In answering the first question, Augustine proposes that the "will to believe" is neither only from free choice nor only from God. He quotes Phil 2:13, "It is God, after all, who produces in us the willing and the action in accord with good will."[196] For this reason, we must say faith is a gift of God. Yet, he also affirms that the will to believe must be received as a gift, "when at God's call it arises from the free choice which they received as part of their nature when they were created."[197] God causes the gift of faith to arise in the will, but the will is a "neutral power that can either turn to faith or fall into unbelief."[198] The will chooses to accept or reject God's gift.

This truth is restated, when Augustine answers his second question, "Why doesn't everyone have the will to believe"? He begins by assuring us that God wills all men to be saved. All are not saved, however, because God is not willing "to deprive them of that freedom of choice, for the good or evil use of which they are subject to the judgment of absolute

---

191. Ibid.
192. Ibid., 32.55
193. Ibid., 33.57.
194. Ibid.
195. Ibid.
196. Ibid.
197. Ibid., 33.58.
198. Ibid.

Justice."[199] Augustine is clearly still affirming the "helping hand" model of grace, where grace is offered to all, but the freedom to say "Yes" or "No" to grace is also given. Those who choose not to believe, "act against the will of God," and "deprive themselves of the great and supreme good and plunge themselves into evils which are punishments."[200] They will be guilty of having "held in contempt" God's mercy.[201] Thus, the answer to the second question is: All do receive the will to believe as a gift from God, but many choose to reject this gift and act against God's will, depriving themselves of the gift God desired to give them.

Augustine again assures his readers this explanation does not weaken Paul's words from 1 Cor 4:7, "What do you have that you have not received?"[202] The will to believe is God's gift, "because God brings it about by the enticements of our perceptions that we will and that we believe."[203] He does this through both external and internal means, which humans do not control, "though to assent or dissent is in the power of the will."[204] The will does not believe by free choice alone, but must be enticed or invited to believe by God. Augustine summarizes, "God produces in them the will to believe, but to assent to God's invitation or to dissent from it is, as I said, in the power of one's will."[205] This explanation is in agreement with 1 Corinthians 4:7, because the soul receives and has the gifts of God "only by assenting."[206]

Wetzel says, in both *To Simplician* and *Spirit and the Letter*, "the one inalienable contribution that human beings make to their own redemption is the consent they give to the divine influence at work within them."[207] As we examine the text of *Spirit and the Letter*, we find support for Wetzel's analysis. Augustine tells us God's gifts are received "only by assenting," and whatever good gifts the soul receives, "comes from God,

---

199. Ibid.
200. Ibid.
201. Ibid.
202. Ibid., 34.60.
203. Ibid.
204. Ibid.
205. Ibid.
206. Ibid.
207. Wetzel, "Pelagius," 130.

but the receiving and the having certainly come from the one who receives and has them."[208]

In conclusion, we can say, then, the gift of faith comes from God alone, as it arises within the free choice of the will, but the will is a neutral power that can choose to receive and have this gift by assenting, or reject this gift and hold God's mercy in contempt by dissenting. Augustine has returned to the position we saw in his early works, where *gratia* is given to all, then humans make a decision of their will to believe or disbelieve the promises of God. All who believe are given *adiutorium* to help them do good works.

In *Spirit and the Letter*, Augustine firmly upholds the will's freedom to reject grace and disbelieve the gospel. Grace entices and invites the will to believe, but it does not impose necessity. Bonner writes, "Augustine is clear that, in this life, grace does not override free will. Under the action of Divine Grace, the will remains its own master. It can accept or refuse the call of God."[209] Rist underlines the importance of this freedom, "Unless the saints have the option to reject the advances of the spirit, their freedom under grace is a cruel sham."[210] Burns agrees, "If the reality of consent to receive, and the possibility of refusal, be denied, there is an end to any understanding of grace as a loving relation between persons."[211] For love to be real, it is necessary that the beloved have the right to refuse the advance of his lover. In *Spirit and the Letter*, Augustine upholds the freedom of the will to say "No" to the invitation of grace.

This concludes our study of Augustine's middle works, where he has significantly modified his doctrine of election. In *To Simplician*, he rejected faith as the basis for election. God's good pleasure became the only basis for his choice. The introduction of the concept of *massa peccati* liberated God from any juridical constraints to be gracious to all men. Yet, Augustine clings to his early theory of moral responsibility and the traditional interpretation of 1 Tim 2:4, so that he is looking for some basis in the human will for the damnation of the reprobate. The crucial balance he strikes in *Spirit and the Letter* is the proposition that reprobation is the consequence of man's saying "No" to God's gift of faith. Those who reject

---

208. Augustine, *Spirit and the Letter*, 34.60.
209. Bonner, *Controversies*, 385.
210. Rist, "Predestination," 422.
211. Burns, *Development*, 230.

this gift act against the will of God and deprive themselves of his mercy by dissenting from his grace. Augustine's vacillating theories of will show us the difficulty he is having balancing free will and unconditional election. In the middle works he attempts to balance them by affirming the will's power to say "No" to grace, but this is inconsistent with his doctrine of unconditional election. In his later works, he will deny the will's power to say "No," and fully embrace the causally determined will. Efficacious grace and unconditional election will soon conquer his early notion of free will and his balance will shift completely toward grace.

Chapter 3

Augustine's Later Works

It is in the latter stage of Augustine's career that we see the most significant changes in his doctrines of grace and human willing, so we must carefully examine his later works. To better grasp how his thoughts develop we will study these works chronologically, as much as possible, although this presents challenges, considering the date each work is completed is not always incontestable. Rist warns of the difficulty of a chronological study, "important evidence for his key beliefs is often widely scattered; arguments are left incomplete and revived years later; problems are raised and pushed aside."[1] Following these works chronologically leads us on some detours, as Augustine seeks to understand grace and willing in ways that are consistent with his doctrine of unconditional election. He is also engaged in the Pelagian controversy, where rhetoric is heated and his opponents are frequently citing his early works in opposition to his later works, so this journey is full of twists, turns, and even some backtracking. Yet, this methodology allows us to see how Augustine works through the struggle to balance free will and moral responsibility with God's sovereignty in election and redemption.

Nature and Grace

Augustine wrote *Nature and Grace* to respond to Pelagius's book *On Nature*, which conceded man's need for grace, even if it was a rather limited notion of grace. The section of *Nature and Grace* most pertinent to our study is Augustine's response to Pelagius's use of quotations from *Free Will*. Pelagius accepted Augustine's definition of sin, as a voluntary act of

1. Rist, *Augustine*, 10.

the will and especially liked the declaration, "Whatever the cause of the will is, if one cannot resist it, one yields to it without sin."[2] Augustine admits those were his words, but now, interprets them to embrace a "cause of the will" toward sin that can be resisted with the help of grace. He does not explain why the reprobate are guilty of sin, though original sin causes them to sin and grace is withheld. He restates his conclusion from *Free Will*, that the penal condition of ignorance and difficulty is not counted as sin, unless our wills "hold in contempt" the one who wants to heal us.[3] He appears to be both affirming and denying moral responsibility for necessary sin. His belief that moral responsibility must be tied to the free choice of the will, is now colliding with his doctrine of original sin, which is his sole means of justifying the unconditional election of the reprobate to hell. He is still searching for the answer to the question that has eluded him since *To Simplician*, "Why did God hate the reprobate before they did any evil?" He recognizes it cannot be because he foreknows their future evil actions or election would not be unconditional. He suggests they are hated for Adam's sin but acknowledges that only Adam's will was involved in that sin. The link between free choice and moral responsibility, which had been so important in his early works, appears to only be true for the unique case of Adam. Natural and necessary sin are part of the penal condition of all Adam's descendants, though he struggles to explain how this can be just.

Perfection of Human Righteousness and Deeds of Pelagius

Perfection of Human Righteousness shows us some of the challenges with Augustine's darkened view of man's fallen condition. Caelestius asks him whether sin can be avoided, arguing that if it cannot it is not sin. Augustine replies, "We answer that sin can be avoided, if our injured nature is healed by grace."[4] Those who are denied grace are, nonetheless, judged guilty for unavoidable sin. Caelestius asks if sin arises from necessity or from will, believing that if it is from necessity, it cannot be sin. Augustine points to the psalmist's prayer for the Lord to deliver him from

---

2. Augustine, *Nature and Grace*, 67.80.
3. Ibid., 67.81.
4. Ibid., 2.2.

his necessities.[5] The clear implication is that necessary sin is still sin for which we are culpable. This is a major departure from his early teachings, as well as the teachings of previous church fathers. Most accepted the mortality we inherited from Adam as an explanation for our sinfulness, but this involved a tendency or an inclination toward sin, not necessary sinning.[6] Irenaeus said, whatever we inherit from Adam, we remain free within limits to choose between good and evil.[7] Origen taught that every rational soul had free will and choice. Spiritual powers will urge us to sin or help us toward salvation but in neither case are we compelled by necessity.[8] John Chrysostom instructed that the fall of Adam did not remove human freedom to choose the good. He also said that mortality was not the cause of sin and was no hindrance to virtue.[9] Theodore of Mopsuestia wrote that only nature could be inherited and not sin, since sin implies the disobedience of the free unrestrained will.[10]

Augustine sets himself apart from these theologians by teaching, there was in fallen man, a total incapacity for virtue.[11] He has come to believe that Adam's descendants are born in a penal state, where sin is necessary from birth. Several times he quotes Luke 18:19, "No one is good except God alone."[12] A letter he wrote to Jerome about this time, however, reveals some discomfort he was having with his developing theory of original sin. He writes, "how can it be just of the Creator to bind them by another's sin, when they are joined to mortal bodies descended from him, so that damnation is their lot"?[13] G. R. Evans explains, "Augustine recognized a classic difficulty here. It is easy to see how original sin may be transmitted to the soul if all souls are derived from the soul of Adam, as all human bodies are derived from his body. It is far from easy to explain the matter if we argue that all souls are freshly created."[14]

---

5. Augustine, *Perfection of Human Righteousness*, 2.2.
6. Greer, "Sinned We All," 338.
7. Ibid., 385.
8. Bostock, "Origen: The Alternative to Augustine?," 329.
9. Greer, "Sinned We All," 387.
10. Ibid., 388.
11. Ibid., 390.
12. Augustine, *Perfection*, 14.32.
13. Augustine, *Letter 166*, 10.1.
14. Evans, *Augustine on Evil*, 124.

Augustine seeks to soften the blow of original sin by urging that the necessary healing grace is offered to all. He says, "He [God] sets them free from the evil . . . if they will it, believe, and call upon him."[15] Grace is available to "those who make progress by willing and believing and calling upon God."[16] Both in its initial actions and in its continuation, grace appears to be conditionally given to those who seek it, will it, and believe it. He cites many Scripture texts that affirm man's power to choose between good and evil, again returning to his early assumption that moral responsibility is contingent on the will being free to choose between moral alternatives. He exhorts people to pray for God's mercy and grace, since, "It is not that it is done without our will, but that our will does not accomplish what it does unless it is helped by God."[17] Augustine is again returning to the "helping hand" model of grace.

Augustine says, men must "seek the one who would set them free and save them."[18] He writes, "people are not helped unless they themselves do something. But they are helped if they call upon God, if they believe, if they have been called in accord with God's plan . . . And this healing is produced with our cooperation by the grace of God through Jesus Christ, our Lord."[19] Some scholars suggest these quotes only describe how grace works in the life of a believer. This is doubtful, however, since he calls men to seek the one who can "set them free and save them."[20] Throughout *Perfection of Human Righteousness*, he presents a grace that, both prior to and after salvation, works in response to the prayers and choices of human beings.

In *Deed of Pelagius*, probably written in late 417, Augustine accepts Pelagius's claim that Paul taught grace was given on the basis of faith, not on the basis of works, but asserts, "we have not merited to have this faith by any faith."[21] He asks, "Have we given it to ourselves and made ourselves believers"?[22] He is revisiting the question from *Spirit and the Letter*, which asked where the will to believe came from. He concluded

15. Augustine, *Perfection*, 4.10.
16. Ibid., 5.11.
17. Ibid., 19.40.
18. Ibid., 19.42.
19. Ibid., 20.43.
20. Ibid., 19.42.
21. Augustine, *Deeds of Pelagius*, 15.34.
22. Ibid.

then, that it was a gift of God which arose in the free choice of the will and could be received or rejected by the assent or dissent of the will. In *Deeds of Pelagius*, he continues to call faith a gift of God, but by asking if we make ourselves believers and answering, "He made us; we did not make ourselves,"[23] he is downplaying the role of the will which was crucial in *Spirit and the Letter*. We see the shape of things to come here, as he moves toward his mature view that faith, like creation, is an act of God alone.

Grace of Christ and Original Sin

Grace of Christ and Original Sin was written in 418, after Pelagius sent a letter to Pope Zosimus that was full of references to grace.[24] Pelagius admitted grace was necessary, "not only at every hour and at every moment, but also for every act of ours."[25] Augustine objects that Pelagius's *In Defense of Free Choice* had distinguished three things by which we obey God's commands: the ability, the will, and the action. Though he says the ability was God's gift, Augustine alleges he would not admit the same thing for the will or the action.[26] He reasons, "We should certainly realize that he does not believe that either our will or our action is aided by God's help, but only the ability for willing and for acting."[27] He again quotes Phil 2:13, highlighting that God produces "the willing and the acting, which Pelagius insists are due to us, as if they were not helped by divine grace."[28]

Augustine is probably correct in his interpretation of *In Defense of Free Choice*, but in his letter to the pope, Pelagius proposes a grace that is very similar to the "helping hand" model Augustine has proposed on several occasions. "He (God) produces in us a willing that is good, a willing that is holy," writes Pelagius. "He does this by rousing the sluggish will to a desire for God through revealing his wisdom; he does this by urging us toward everything that is good."[29] These concessions, however, are not enough for Augustine. He now stipulates that grace must be operative or

23. Ibid.
24. Rotelle, "Introduction to *Grace and Free Choice*," 358.
25. Augustine, *Grace of Christ*, 1.2.2.
26. Ibid., 1.3.4.
27. Ibid., 1.5.6.
28. Ibid.
29. Ibid., 1.10.11.

efficacious and not just helpful: "But we want the Pelagians at some point to admit not merely the grace by which we are promised the great glory to come, but that by which we believe in and hope for it; not merely the grace by which wisdom is revealed, but that by which we love it as well; not merely the grace by which we are urged on toward everything good, but that which moves us to action."[30]

Augustine rejects Pelagius's grace that rouses the will, reveals wisdom, and urges toward good. Instead, he mandates an effectual grace, which "helps the willing itself"[31] and produces the assent of the will.

TeSelle asserts, the *locus classicus* of the dramatic change in Augustine's theory of free will is found in *Grace of Christ*, when he writes, "This grace not only makes us know what we should do, but also makes us do what we know; it not only makes us believe what we should love, but makes us love what we believe . . . In that way he not merely reveals the truth, but also imparts love. After all, that is the way God teaches those who have been called according to his purpose."[32]

The congruent call of *To Simplician* is being replaced by a more powerful grace, that does not wait for the will's assent, but actually causes the assent of the will. Burns contends this new concept of grace allows for the "bestowing of new dispositions and the giving of willing itself."[33] Now, grace "makes us do," "makes us believe," and "makes us love" what God has ordained. Burns explains that Augustine's, "argument for the necessity of grace asserted that charity does not simply strengthen a desire and facilitate its performance; it effectively orients a person's intention in a new direction."[34] Wetzel quotes Jean Lebourlier's summary of this extraordinary reversal on grace's *modus operandi*, "Callings are no longer given to suit the disposition of those called; those called are instead given the disposition to accept their callings."[35]

In contrast to what he had concluded in *Spirit and the Letter*, Augustine now instructs that the good will comes from God alone and not from ourselves. He dismisses Pelagius's concession, saying, "He must think that

---

30. Ibid.
31. Ibid., 1.14.15.
32. Augustine, *Grace of Christ*, 1.12.23—13.14.
33. Burns, *Development*, 144–5.
34. Ibid., 141.
35. Wetzel, *Virtue*, 187–8.

good will is something other than the love which, as Scripture cries out, comes to us from God and has been given to us by the Father so that we might be his children."[36] He also rejects Pelagius's claim that fallen man must be able to choose between good and evil alternatives to be morally responsible. This is a startling reversal of his own teaching, as recently as *Perfection of Human Righteousness*, that the will is a "neutral power," which chooses between good and evil.

For Augustine, the root or source of our actions is no longer the *possibilitas utriusque partis*, or "freedom of decision," but the fundamental orientation of the soul toward either *caritas* (love) or *cupiditas* (lust).[37] This orientation limits the choices available to the will. TeSelle explains, "Willing, wherever it is found, is freedom within a certain horizon of necessity."[38] Augustine has come to believe the fallen will is completely motivated by lust and operates within the horizon of necessary sin, with no freedom to choose good. Original sin has become the cause of the will's necessary assent to evil and grace has become the cause of its assent to good. In neither case does the will determine itself.

Portalié urges us to believe, "Augustine never retracted his principal ideas on freedom of choice; he never modified his thought on the factor which is its essential condition, that is, its complete power of choosing or determining itself."[39] If Portalié means to say that Augustine continues to affirm freedom of choice which operates within a limited horizon of necessity, then there is support for his view. However, the phrase, "complete power of choosing and determining itself" is inaccurate. Augustine no longer believes the will has freedom to choose between good and evil like a hinge. He claims, "we are drawn neither to virtue nor to vice by necessity," but then concedes this is only true when, "with the help of grace . . . the evil necessity will be removed, and full freedom will be given to us."[40] In other words, without grace, men *are* drawn to vice by necessity. Portalié's claim, "There is not a single one of his later anti-Pelagian works in which Augustine does not positively proclaim the complete power of

---

36. Augustine, *Grace of Christ*, 1.21.22.
37. TeSelle, *Augustine the Theologian*, 292.
38. Ibid.
39. Portalié, *Guide*, 197.
40. Augustine, *Nature and Grace*, 65.78.

choice," must be accompanied by his own admission that for Augustine, "God has the absolute power of directing this choice."[41]

Augustine exhorts Pelagius to agree that God helps the will "in such a way that we will or do nothing good without that help."[42] He urges, "only the charity which the Holy Spirit gives actually moves a person to the love of God."[43] The "good will" and the "will to believe" are now seen as aspects of the "love of God," which is "not that by which he loves us, but that by which he makes us love him."[44] This is a key development. The phrase, "love of God," has come to mean, for Augustine, the way in which God "makes us love him." He is not using this phrase to describe God's wooing of man's will, while waiting for humans to respond in kind. Rather it is a unilateral action of God upon the will that infuses the will with the "love of God" and "makes us love him." The will's assent to this transformation is caused by the infusion of love. Effectual grace makes the wills of the elect love God.

Augustine believes effectual grace is necessary because the fallen will lacks any power to choose good no matter how much it is helped. The evil will cannot choose good until after it has been converted into a good will. Effectual grace transforms the evil will making it good and making it love God. Marianne Djuth explains that the fallen will has lost the *possibilitas boni* (the possibility of goodness) and therefore its power of choice has been completely corrupted, so that choice cannot function.[45] Without the possibility of goodness, the will lacks the "complete power of choice" articulated by Portalié and has only the corrupted choice described by Djuth. It "freely" chooses evil until it is caused to "freely" choose good. The will is always necessarily moved in one direction or the other and never has the freedom to choose between these moral alternatives.

Augustine's conviction that man cannot choose good apart from God's causal influence was fortified by his blending of the doctrine of "creation from nothing" with the Neo-Platonism he learned from Plotinus. This combination led him to conclude that man is a being made out of temporal, unstable, and corruptible substance that, without divine aid,

---

41. Portalié, *Guide*, 197.
42. Augustine, *Grace of Christ*, 1.47.52.
43. Burns, *Development*, 112.
44. Augustine, *Spirit and the Letter*, 33.56.
45. Djuth, "Hermeneutics," 287.

always tends to fall back toward nothingness.[46] When this philosophy is applied to questions of the human will and grace, Augustine gravitates toward effectual or operative grace. Since God is the only source of good in the universe, he alone can move man to choose good. In fact, Harrison suggests that from creation, even prior to the fall, man must necessarily have been incapable of any good without grace. She writes, "The radical, ontological dualism of creation from nothing, which placed the external, immutable and omnipotent Creator on one side of reality and a finite, mutable, absolutely dependent creation upon the other, served to cut through the substantial dualism of Manichaeism and the ethical dualism of Pelagianism with equal force, by emphasizing the utter contingency of creation upon its Creator."[47] Harrison continues, "It is as if created reality has an inherent tendency to fall away from God, not just ethically, but ontologically. Grace is therefore not something that suddenly becomes necessary because of human sinfulness, but is part of what defines the relation of Creator and creature . . . The fall is not, therefore, primarily the fall of Adam and Eve but the inherent tendency of created reality to fall away from its Creator and to fall back to the nothingness from which it came."[48]

John Hick indicates that being made from nothingness is like being made from "a material of inferior quality," which makes man inherently unstable.[49] Even in paradise, it was impossible for man to be good unless he was infused with the divine presence, which is grace.[50] Augustine's Christianized Plotinian view assumes that without divine light and love the creation lapses into nothingness.[51] Grace is the only force stopping man's fall into nothingness and sin. This evolved view of grace fits well with the unconditional election presented in *To Simplician*. God is the source of all goodness, and unconditional election is the distribution of this goodness to whomever he wills. Those who fall away from him toward nothingness and evil are unable to change direction and love him, unless the Holy Spirit distributes the love of God to them. Augustine

46. Harrison, *Rethinking*, 99.
47. Ibid., 82.
48. Ibid., 92.
49. Hick, *Evil and the God of Love*, 52.
50. Bonner, "Anti-Pelagian Works," 41.
51. Burns, "Grace," 392.

continues to defend free choice but is obligated to adjust his definition of what it means. The will is not free to choose whether it will be good or evil, since "we obtain a good will from God."[52] The will "freely" chooses between evil options unless grace makes it "freely" choose good.

Letter 194 and Answer to the Two Letters of the Pelagians

The same year Augustine wrote *Grace of Christ and Original Sin*, he also wrote *Letter 194* to Pope Sixtus, which Wetzel claims completely overturned the theory of the congruent call proposed in *To Simplician*.[53] *Letter 194* alleges that God does more than simply call the fallen will in a way that suits it. Instead, he renovates the will by removing sinful desires and replacing them with the desire for God and good. This shift in Augustine's concept of the call is accompanied by a devaluation of man's condition *sub lege* (under the law and not yet under grace), until the will is denuded of all redeeming desires and man is incapable of any good at all without the aid of grace. Wetzel surmises, Augustine "has to move to an ever more radical internal operation for the simple reason that grace must answer an ever more radical condition of perversity."[54]

Burns posits that as of 418, Augustine held to four key propositions: First, the necessity of divine assistance to fulfill the conditions for salvation; Second, the inability of a person to fulfill the conditions that would qualify him for this divine assistance; Third, this divine assistance gives a person not only the capacity to act but also a "tendency to performance" without overriding human free choice; Fourth, grace is given that guarantees salvation and perseverance, by not only enabling and helping performance, but by actually causing it.[55] Burns recognizes the fourth principle overrides the third. It was added, he says, because of Augustine's evolved view of a "radical impotence in the human nature," such that even if it is given an impetus or tendency toward performance, it will eventually fail. He concurs with Harrison, that this radical impotence is a corollary of Augustine's comprehension of man being created out of nothing.[56] Wil-

---

52. Augustine, *Punishment and Forgiveness*, 2.18.30.
53. Wetzel, *Virtue*, 187–8.
54. Ibid.
55. Burns, *Development*, 122.
56. Ibid.

liam Mann agrees that for Augustine, "creatures have a natural tendency toward mutability and corruption, an unavoidable liability of their having been created *ex nihilo*."[57] Men inevitably fall into sin and nothingness, unless grace fills them with divine love.

Augustine had previously taught that the soul was converted as it assented to the influence of grace and was then infused with *caritas*.[58] In his later works, "Augustine began to think of grace as an inward influence from the very beginning of the process of conversion."[59] The love of God is poured into the human heart causing assent. The consent of the will is no longer necessary before conversion. This new concept of operative grace excludes human autonomy from the conversion process. Consent no longer comes from ourselves, but it is the product of grace.

Augustine's doctrine of election has remained consistent since he adopted unconditional election in *To Simplician*, but it has consistently propelled him to change his view of grace. He based his changes on the notion he initially proposed in *To Simplician*, that God "bestows voluntary assent."[60] Burns says, in the initial phase of the Pelagian controversy, Augustine had urged the necessity of grace, yet upheld human autonomy, "at least in the roles of accepting, activating and preserving the power God gives," however, in 418, he "abandoned the defense of freedom and argued the efficacy of both charity and the grace of faith."[61]

Letter 194 sent shock waves through the monastery at Hadrumetum and provoked a crisis atmosphere among the monks. In this letter, Augustine declares that "a human being cannot have a good will without the help of God."[62] "Good works are, to be sure, produced by a human being," he says, "but faith is produced in a human being."[63] He asks, "if we say that faith, by which one would merit grace, came first, what merit did a human being have before faith in order to receive faith?"[64] God produces faith in the human vessel, causing the will's consent. Burns claims this is "an

---

57. Mann, "Evil," 44.
58. TeSelle, *Augustine the Theologian*, 332.
59. Ibid., 333.
60. Augustine, *To Simplician*, 1.2.21.
61. Burns, *Development*, 126.
62. Augustine, *Letter 194*, 2.3
63. Ibid., 3.9.
64. Ibid., 3.15.

assertion of direct influence on the will itself through an interior grace."[65] In Augustine's own words, "The help of the Holy Spirit is described in such a way, therefore, that he is said to do what he makes us do."[66]

In *Letter 194*, Augustine reaffirmed his doctrine of unconditional election based on two pillars. These were infant baptism and the case of Jacob and Esau in Romans 9. He insists those who complain about God's partiality in election, "lose all the force of their human arguments when it comes to infants."[67] He sees no other explanation for why some infants survive long enough to be baptized, while others do not, except that God hated some and loved others. Turning to Romans 9, he asks, "And what did he [God] hate in Esau before he was born and had done anything bad but original sin?"[68] God hates all men for Adam's sin alone, before they have any personal sins, but he chooses to love, forgive, and have mercy on some, while choosing to persevere in his hatred for others.

In *Answer to the Two Letters of the Pelagians*, Augustine offers revised definitions of "free choice," "freedom," and "free will." He says "free choice" was not removed from humanity after Adam's sin. "In fact, all people sin by their free choice,"[69] though without grace their free choice is limited to evil. Portalié says, "Leaving aside original sin . . . every personal sin is essentially free according to Augustine and presumes the complete power of not committing it."[70] While it is true that Augustine considered all personal sins to be the result of "free choice," it is not true that he "presumes the complete power of not committing it." This was true under his early definition, but in *Answer to the Two Letter of the Pelagians* he declares, "They are free from righteousness only by the choice of the will."[71] That is, "free choice" is free from being able to choose righteousness and is only free to choose evil.

"Freedom," which existed in paradise, perished with Adam's sin. Portalié explains, "this liberty which was lost is not the power to choose between good and evil as one pleases . . . It is rather that original

---

65. Burns, *Development*, 9.
66. Augustine, *Letter 194*, 4.16.
67. Ibid., 7.31.
68. Ibid., 8.34.
69. Augustine, *Two Letters*, 1.2.5.
70. Portalié, *Guide*, 226.
71. Augustine, *Two Letters*, 1.2.5.

perfection of the will freeing it from concupiscence."⁷² Creswell says, Augustine changed the definitions of "freedom" and "free will," from "being autonomous" to "being liberated."⁷³ The man who has "freedom" or "free will" has been set free from lust and is now motivated by the "love of God" to do good. This is a clear departure from the classical definition of "free will," as well as Augustine's own early definition. Citing Rom 6:20–22, Augustine lays out his new distinction between "free choice" and "free will." The one who has "free choice" is a slave to sin and is free from righteousness. The one who has "free will" is set free from sin and is a slave to God.⁷⁴

When Julian accuses him of teaching that all are "forced" into sin by the constraints of the flesh, Augustine insists that man's choice to sin comes from his own will. Yet, he also admits, "this will which is free for evil actions because it takes delight in evil is not free for good actions, because it has not been set free."⁷⁵ He declares, "none are forced by the power of God against their will either to do evil or to do good, but if God abandons them, they turn toward evil . . . if God helps them, they are turned toward good."⁷⁶ The reprobate are abandoned by God and never given the will to turn toward good. The wills of the elect are "turned toward good" in an effectual way, which they cannot resist.

To Julian's charge that he taught fatalism, Augustine responds that believing God's grace precedes all human merit is not the same as fate.⁷⁷ Again he points to infant baptism and asks why some babies get baptized, while others do not. "There is no fate," he says, "because there is the grace of God, and there is no partiality, because there is the grace of God."⁷⁸ For Augustine, the fact God decides what will happen removes fatalism. He reminds Julian that Romans 9 teaches some people are made for dishonorable purposes. God's grace helps those whom he has chosen to be vessels of mercy, while his judgment serves as a lesson to those whom he has chosen to be vessels of wrath. "The benefit which is gratuitously given

---

72. Portalié, *Guide*, 224.
73. Creswell, *Dilemma*, 117.
74. Augustine, *Two Letters*, 1.2.5.
75. Ibid., 1.3.7.
76. Ibid., 1.18.36.
77. Ibid., 2.5.9.
78. Ibid., 2.6.11.

to some would not be clearly seen, unless to others from that same mass, persons equally guilty and condemned to just punishment, God showed what both of them deserved."[79]

In a crucial passage, Augustine proposes, "Now the point to which we must turn our attention is whether God breathes into an unwilling and resisting human being the desire for good so that one no longer resists and is no longer unwilling, but consents to the good and wills the good." His answer is unequivocally "Yes!" He cites 2 Cor 3:5, "It is not that we are able to think of something as if coming from ourselves; rather our ability comes from God," and interprets it to mean, "that we are not able . . . to think of something good as if coming from ourselves."[80] Since nothing good comes from ourselves, then our will's consent to good cannot come from ourselves. It must come from God. This interpretation may distort the context of the verse, but it is used repeatedly in his later works to prove man's inability to will anything good, unless God causes him to do so. When the Pelagians cite Prov 16:1, "It is up to a human being to prepare the heart," Augustine quotes what is probably an old Latin version of Prov 8:35, "The will is prepared by the Lord."[81] This is a poor translation of the verse, but Augustine uses it more than fifty times as a proof text for his evolved notion that God is the author of all good willing.

Augustine has now fully adopted a compatibilist view similar to the Stoics, who said there was no contradiction between necessity and free will.[82] He writes, "Hence God does many good things in human beings that the human beings do not do, but human beings do nothing good that God does not make them do."[83] Rist warns that this mature theory of how grace produces the will leaves even the elect individual as "no more than an animated puppet."[84] Some may object to this inflammatory language, but Augustine himself has frequently stated God "makes" humans have a good will, believe, and do good. The last portion of the quote above, "human beings do nothing good that God does not make them do," appears to validate Rist's dark opinion. For Augustine, the good will is created by

---

79. Ibid., 2.7.15.
80. Ibid., 2.8.18.
81. Ibid., 2.9.19–20.
82. Djuth, "Stoicism," 391.
83. Augustine, *Two Letters*, 2.9.21.
84. Rist, "Augustine," 429.

a unilateral action of God that does not come from us in any way. He has rejected the libertarian concept of free will found in his early works and has substituted Stoic compatibilism.[85]

The changes in Augustine's concepts of grace and free will are logical consequences of his doctrine of unconditional election combined with the commonly held Neo-Platonic understanding of God's immutability. Plato taught that the most perfect thing was the most self-sufficient, which could not be changed by things outside itself.[86] Augustine believed that God decided in eternity all that would be done in every moment of time. This precludes any possibility that God responds or reacts to temporal human wills. To insure that all he has predestined comes to pass, God orders the wills of men, so that they do only what he has ordained.

Burns believes Augustine's doctrine of grace evolved in three stages: "In *De gratia Christi* (*Grace of Christ*), Augustine opposed Pelagius's understanding of grace as exterior teaching by asserting the efficacy of the interior instruction in faith and charity. In *Epistula 194* (*Letter 194*) to Sixtus, he assigned the entire process of conversion to the operation of the Holy Spirit. Then in *Contra duas epistulas Pelagianorum* (*Answer to the Two Letters of the Pelagians*), he demonstrated that the grace of conversion actually reverses a person's resistance to God."[87]

This is the most significant revelation in *Answer to the Two Letters of the Pelagians*. God is said to breathe the desire for good into unwilling and resisting humans, so that they no longer resist but become willing instead. The Pelagians accused him of teaching that grace "injects a desire for virtue" into those who were unwilling.[88] They questioned the legitimacy of this unilateral transformation, which changed the unwilling person into a willing person without their consent and allowing no possibility of dissent.

Answer to Julian, Enchiridion, and City of God

In book 1 of *Answer to Julian*, written about 421, Augustine says a nature is created by God and is good, though it is capable of good and evil. It is

---

85. Djuth, "Stoicism," 387.
86. Edwards, "Pagan Dogma," 309.
87. Burns, *Development*, 142.
88. Augustine, *Two Letters*, 2.10.22.

capable of good as it participates in God's goodness, and it is capable of evil by a "privation of good."[89] He cites Matt 7:18, "A good tree does not produce bad fruit," and says, "one should understand that the bad tree is a bad will, because there is a falling away from the highest good, when the created good is deprived of the creative good so that the root of evil in the created good is nothing but lack of good. But the good tree is the good will precisely because a human being is through it turned back to the highest and immutable good and is filled with the good so that it produces good fruit."[90]

This passage reveals two of the foundational assumptions for Augustine's developing theories of grace and human willing. The first is his conviction that evil is a "privation of good." This notion sees God as the only source of good in the universe. Good exists in the world only when God produces it, and no other entity can produce good or the universe would be made better than God created it. Augustine writes, "God is the author of all goods, that is, of good natures and of good wills, for only God, not a human being, produces the good will in a human being."[91] This view of good leads him to a unique perspective on evil. "The root of evil" is nothing but the lack of God's goodness. The bad will occurs when the created good (man) is deprived of the creative good (God). The remedy for this falling away is being filled with the creative good, which is an action only God can initiate. If one accepts this premise, it leads to the conclusion that there is no role the created good can play in its own goodness. Man is totally dependent on God's decision to either grant or deprive him of goodness. The troubling aspect of this premise is that it makes all evil in the universe, ultimately, the result of God's decision to withhold his goodness. The universe is only as good as God wanted it to be. We will explore this further as we proceed.

Augustine's second assumption is that human wills are either driven by good motives or by bad motives. The divided will of *Confessions* is nowhere to be found. Now, he assumes that every will is either a good will, motivated by love, or a bad will, motivated by lust. "The tree is the will, whether good or evil, and its actions are its fruit . . . A bad will does not

---

89. Augustine, *Answer to Julian*, 1.8.37.
90. Ibid., 1.9.45.
91. Ibid.

produce good actions, and a good will does not produce bad actions."[92] This assumption oversimplifies the human condition, since Christians continue to struggle with sin and unbelievers do good deeds. It also makes it difficult, if not impossible, for Augustine to explain why Adam's good will chose to sin. Nonetheless, he clings to it because it is complementary to his theory of effectual grace.

Augustine's belief God is the sole mover in redemption, so that the human will has no role, leads Julian to complain that he is limiting the love and mercy of God. The absence of human good will has no other cause than God's own will to deprive men of goodness and grace, which would contradict 1 Tim 2:4, "who wills that all human beings be saved and come to the knowledge of the truth."[93] Augustine again points to infant baptism. "Why then does God, who wills that all human beings be saved and come to the knowledge of the truth, permit that so many who do not resist him by the choice of their will not come into his kingdom?"[94] Augustine has come to believe that God does not will to save all. He offers an alternate translation of 1 Tim 2:4, "For God wills that all those be saved and come to the knowledge of the truth to whom grace comes."[95]

Julian also wonders what value there is to asking, seeking, and knocking if God does not respond to human willing. Augustine looks to infant baptism again and recounts how infants, "scream, spit and fight back, and yet they receive, find, and have the door opened for them.[96] His point is that grace is not God's response to human seeking, asking, or knocking, but rather, a gift given in spite of human resistance. His logic may be inescapable, if one accepts the premise that infant baptism saves. Burnaby claims, "Apart from Scripture and the Church's practice of infant baptism, his argument against Julian, rests almost entirely upon the sufferings of children too young 'to have sins of their own.'"[97] Augustine admits, "This question, in which the dispute concerns the choice of the will and the grace of God, is so difficult to sort out that, when one defends free choice, one seems to deny God's grace, and when one upholds God's

92. Ibid., 1.8.38.
93. Ibid., 4.8.42.
94. Ibid.
95. Ibid.
96. Ibid.
97. Burnaby, *Amor*, 203.

grace, one is thought to destroy free choice."⁹⁸ It is a comfort to realize that even an intellect as great as Augustine's, found this issue difficult to grasp.

About the same time he wrote *Answer to Julian*, Augustine also wrote the *Enchiridion*, which was one of the earliest and most influential systematic theologies written during the patristic period.⁹⁹ He again quotes Matt 12:33, "Either make the tree good, and its fruit good; or make the tree bad, and its fruit bad."¹⁰⁰ This exhortation seems at odds with his denial of man's freedom to choose between good and evil. He restates the importance of human assent, writing, "But if assent is taken away, faith is taken away, since nothing can be believed without assent."¹⁰¹ This might appear to be a return to the position he defended in *Spirit and the Letter*, except he now believes that both assent and faith are gifts of God that transform the unwilling into willing.¹⁰² The will lacks any power to choose whether it will be a good tree or a bad tree. God alone decides who will have a good will or a bad will by giving or withholding grace.

When the gift of faith is given, it includes the gift of assent and removes any possibility of dissent. Augustine exclaims, "God does whatever he will, and that would not be true, "if what the Almighty willed was prevented from happening by the will of man.¹⁰³ "The will is prepared by the Lord," in such a way that God, "makes the good will of man ready for his help and helps the will he has made ready." God's mercy "goes before the unwilling, that they may will, and it follows the willing that they may not will in vain."¹⁰⁴ Grace "predisposes a man before he wills, to prompt his willing."¹⁰⁵ Burnaby observes, "And so we find that Augustine will first attribute the forthcomingness of the act of will (*ut velimus*) both to God's calling and to man's response . . . but that in the end the pressure of the controversy will make him assert that it is the forthcomingness of will which God works in us 'without us.'"¹⁰⁶

---

98. Augustine, *Answer to Julian*, 4.8.47.
99. Fiedrowicz, "Introduction," 271.
100. Augustine, *Enchiridion*, 9.30.
101. Ibid., 7.20.
102. Augustine, *Two Letters*, 2.8.17.
103. Augustine, *Enchiridion*, 24.96.
104. Augustine, *Enchiridion*, 9.32.
105. Ibid.
106. Burnaby, *Amor*, 229.

Burnaby is quoting directly from *Grace and Free Choice*, a work written about the same time as *Enchiridion*, where Augustine says, "we will when we will, but he causes us to will what is good . . . He works, therefore, without us so that we will, but when we will and will so that we do an action, he works along with us."[107] In the initial stage of human willing, God is seen as the sole actor, who causes the good will. Once the good will has been produced, then God works with that will to strengthen it. It must be admitted, however, that the human will in no way assents to this initial act of conversion before it happens. It does not have the power of assent until after it has been converted. The assent of the will never precedes conversion but is always produced by God's transformative work on the will at the moment of conversion.

Augustine returns to his favorite two pillars, the baptism of infants[108] and the election of Jacob and Esau in Romans 9, to support his conclusion that God grants grace and faith to whom he wills.[109] "The creator fulfilled what he willed by means of that very will of the creature," who was "in no way able to contravene his will."[110] He adds, "The will of the Almighty is always undefeated."[111] For this reason, he again denies God's universal will to save all and interprets 1 Tim 2:4, "as meaning that nobody is saved except those whom he wills to be saved, not because there is nobody whom he does not will to be saved, but because nobody is saved except those whom he wills to be saved."[112] This is a dramatic revision of his early interpretation of this verse.

Augustine began work on *City of God* around 413 and finished around 427.[113] In book 5, written a few years after *Spirit and the Letter*, he states, "our wills have power to do all that God wanted them to do and foresaw they could do. Their power, such as it is, is a real power."[114] Yet, he also affirms that God's will is all-powerful and "God is the cause of all things."[115] Wetzel claims Augustine makes God's foreknowledge the

---

107. Augustine, *Grace and Free Choice*, 17.33.
108. Augustine, *Enchiridion*, 24.97.
109. Ibid., 25.98.
110. Ibid., 26.100.
111. Ibid., 26.102.
112. Ibid., 27.103.
113. Fitzgerald, "Augustine's Works," xlii.
114. Augustine, *City of God*, 5.9.
115. Ibid.

cause of all that is good, while denying that it is the cause of evil. "What is predestined is foreknown, but not all that is foreknown is predestined."[116]

In book 9, Augustine says all the philosophical schools agree that the mind remains free of the dominations of the passions. He declares, "Even though passions may disturb the inferior part of the soul," the mind remains master over these passions and decides whether to consent to them or resist them.[117] According to Simo Knuuttila, Augustine sees the will is a special faculty that belongs to the superior part of the soul, so that it is able to control the emotions and "in particular can either consent to emotional suggestions or refuse them."[118] Knuuttila reminds us that in both *Trinity* and *Sermon on the Mount*, Augustine's order was: suggestion, passion, then consent. In *Propositions from the Epistle to the Romans*, he said the evil desire was not sin until we consent to it.[119] Again, he appears to be affirming the will's power to say "Yes" or "No" to sinful passions, though this is inconsistent with his more recent writings.

In book 12, Augustine insists that there is no efficient cause of the evil will, asking, "For, what can make the will bad when it is the will itself which makes the action bad?" The bad will, he says, "was made by itself."[120] His belief that the bad will is the cause of evil, leads him to postulate, "Our first parents, then must already have fallen before they could do the evil deed . . . For such 'bad fruit' could come only from a 'bad tree.'"[121] Two questions come to mind: How did Adam and Eve's good wills become evil? Why didn't God's grace preserve their good wills?

As to the latter question, Augustine says, "no one would dare to believe or declare that it was beyond God's power to prevent the fall of either angel or man. But, God, in fact preferred not to use His own power, but to leave success or failure to the creature's choice."[122] God could have given angels and humans enough grace to have prevented their fall, but instead left "success or failure to their choice." In spite of his previous insistence that God's immutability makes it impossible for him to respond or re-

---

116. Wetzel, "Predestination," 50.
117. Augustine, *City of God*, 9.4.
118. Simo Knuuttila, "Emergence," 209.
119. Ibid., 211–3.
120. Augustine, *City of God*, 12.6.
121. Ibid., 14.13.
122. Ibid., 14.27.

act to human willing, he allows for contingency in the fall. These initial choices must be libertarian choices for Adam to be morally responsible for sin. If God foreordained angelic or human sin, then they would not be responsible. Augustine supposes their wills were created good but then fell away from God because of their "creation out of nothing."[123] Harrison hypothesizes that the belief that good comes only from God, implies angels and humans would not have been able to do good without the aid of grace, even before the fall.[124] Augustine affirms this hypothesis when he writes that it was not in man's power to live a good life without the help of God, even in paradise.[125]

In *City of God*, the angels in paradise are also dependent on God for good. Augustine presumes the angels were created with good wills, or otherwise they could have made themselves better than God created them by choosing to be good. This leads us back to the first question of how the good wills of some angels became evil? His extraordinary conclusion is that the angels who fell must have "received less grace of the divine love than did the others, who continued in that grace" or the angels who remained good must have "had greater help to enable them."[126] Babcock says, "the critical point of distinction between the two (good and bad angels) rests in something that God has given to the one and not the other."[127] Since he cannot discover an efficient cause for the fall, Augustine substitutes a deficient cause.[128]

The "origin" of this evil will is the fact that angels are "created out of nothing,"[129] and "things which were made from nothing are capable of deficiency."[130] Though they were created with good wills, "any good will would have been impoverished, remaining in a state of longing, had it not been that he who made, out of nothing, a nature that was good and capable of enjoying him, made it better by fulfilling that desire, first having excited it to greater eagerness for that fulfillment."[131]

123. Ibid., 14.13.
124. Harrison, *Rethinking*, 114.
125. Augustine, *City of God*, 14.27.
126. Ibid., 12.9.
127. Babcock, "Human and the Angelic Fall," 146.
128. Augustine, *City of God*, 12.7.
129. Ibid., 12.6.
130. Ibid., 12.8.
131. Ibid., 12.9.

For their good wills to avoid falling back into nothingness, angels needed a continual infusion of God's grace. The good angels received this grace. "Hence we must believe that the holy angels were never without good will, never that is, without the love of God."[132] It is important to remember this "love of God," which was continually given to the angels, is "not that by which he loves us, but that by which he makes us love him."[133] "Thus we must acknowledge," states Augustine, "that 'the love of God diffused by the Holy Spirit who has been given' does not refer merely to holy men, but is applicable also to the holy angels."[134] Angels who received the diffusion of the "love of God" by the Holy Spirit remained good. Those who did not receive this gift fell away from God. Thus the first evil will, observes Babcock, came about because of "the absence of the full measure of the grace of divine love." He continues, "To the inexplicable conundrum of the good will's turn from the supreme Good, then, Augustine has added the inexplicable mystery of a God who gives and withholds aid without apparent regard for considerations of justice."[135] The evil angels' fall was a result of their having received less grace than the good angels.[136] The cause of their fall was a deficient cause, that is, there was a deficiency in the help they received from God.

Adam appears to have been in a similar condition to the angels. Augustine writes, "Similarly, man in paradise was capable of self-destruction by abandoning justice by an act of will; yet if the life of justice was to be maintained, his will alone would not have sufficed, unless He who made him had given him aid."[137] Adam also needed a continual infusion of the "love of God" to avoid falling and since this gift is effectual, we can assume his fall also came about because grace was deficient to cause his remaining good. This notion of a "deficient cause," seems to imply that the fall was necessary because something was faulty, either in Adam or in the aid he received from God.[138] Rist calls Augustine's contention that Adam had sufficient grace, an "inadequate reply," since he has constantly argued

132. Ibid.
133. Augustine, *Spirit and the Letter*, 33.56.
134. Augustine, *City of God*, 12.9.
135. Babcock, "Human and the Angelic Fall," 147.
136. Ibid., 147.
137. Augustine, *Enchiridion*, 28.106.
138. Rist, *Augustine*, 107.

that the good will aided by sufficient grace always produces good fruit.[139] Adam had no power to keep his will good. So long as he was aided by grace he remained good, but he did not receive grace sufficient to cause him to persevere in goodness.

Gene Fendt suggests this explanation of the fall removes man's will as the *locus* of the fall. It is replaced by the deficiency in the love of God given to Adam and the evil angels.[140] He believes Augustine is willing to accept this conclusion because of his commitment to the proposition that there are some among angels and humans who God simply did not want to help. Augustine denies that God is the efficient cause of the fall in order to avoid making him the author of sin. However, God's choice to withhold effectual grace from Adam and the evil angels was certainly a deliberate choice. Augustine must either abandon his theory that evil is a privation of good or admit that God wanted evil in the world. He chooses the second option, when in the *Enchiridion* he says, God wanted sin in the world, so that his grace, mercy, and justice could be more evident to the world.[141]

Grace and Free Choice, Letter 217, and *Rebuke and Grace*

Augustine explains in *Retractations*, he wrote *Grace and Free Choice* to affirm that one must not deny the grace of God in defending free choice and one must not deny free choice in defending grace.[142] He is writing again to monks in Hadrumetum, who believe that his doctrine of grace denies free choice. The monks quoted his early writings to argue against his new positions. He had written, "It is we who believe and will, but he who gives those believing and willing the ability to do good works through the Holy Spirit."[143] Monks who had admired his early writings, were struggling to divest themselves of this teaching that faith was an act of the will and follow him into his new theology that faith was a gift

---

139. Ibid.
140. Fendt, "Between a Pelagian Rock," 218.
141. Augustine, *Enchiridion*, 28.104.
142. Rotelle, Introduction to *Grace and Free Choice*.
143. Augustine, *Augustine on Romans: Propositions from the Epistle to the Romans*, 61.7.

of God, which causes the assent of the will. Many of the monks simply refused to accept this modification.

Defending his early works, Augustine strongly affirms the free choice of the will, writing, "the divine commandments would not have done human beings any good if they did not have free choice of the will by which they might keep them and come to the promised rewards."[144] "Do not say, 'I have gone astray because of the Lord,'" he warns, "If you are willing, you will keep the commandments and keep good faith with what pleases him . . . whichever they choose will be given to them."[145] He lists many verses, then asks, "What else do they show but the free choice of the human will?"[146] This "free choice" must be helped by grace, but grace does not make the will passive, since Paul begged the Corinthians not to receive the grace of God in vain (2 Cor 6:1). "Why, after all, does he beg them if they received grace in such a way that they lost their own will?" He quotes 1 Cor 15:10, "Not I but the grace of God with me," and observes, "it was neither the grace of God alone nor the apostle alone, but the grace of God with him."[147]

All of this implies a synergy between grace and the believer's will that Augustine has denied in his recent writings. The explanation for this is, the "free choice" he is describing in *Grace and Free Choice,* is that which follows after conversion. He still insists that if anyone is converted, it is "the grace of God alone."[148] The initial decision of faith is not something that originates in our own wills, but is a gift from God alone.[149] TeSelle explains, "The point that is made throughout *On Grace and Free Will* in particular is that everything is the result of grace—but that it must also become human actuality. Augustine even thinks that men ought to pray for the giving of grace, both to others and to themselves, and that prayer and decision and effort are all a part of the process of salvation."[150]

While Augustine believes human willing and action are essential in the process of salvation, it is important to remember that this willing and

---

144. Augustine, *Grace and Free Choice*, 2.2.
145. Ibid., 2.3.
146. Ibid., 2.4.
147. Ibid., 5.12.
148. Ibid.
149. Ibid.,7.17.
150. TeSelle, *Augustine the Theologian*, 327.

action are produced in a human at conversion. Prior to conversion, the will never assents to grace, but is always resistant to it. Grace produces the assent of the will in an unwilling person. Augustine writes,

> It is certain that we will when we will, but he causes us to will what is good, of whom were said the words I cited a little before, "The will is prepared by the Lord." Of him it was said, "The Lord will direct the steps of human beings, and they will choose his path" (Ps. 37:23); of him it was said, "It is God who produces in you the willing as well" (Phil. 2:13). It is certain that we do an action when we do it, but he who says, "I shall make you walk in my ordinances and observe and carry out my judgments" (Ex. 36:27), makes us do the action by offering fully efficacious strength to the will.[151]

Augustine summarizes, "He works, therefore, without us so that we will, but when we will and will so that we do the action, he works along with us."[152] This is a clear statement of his evolved theology of grace, which works "without us" to convert us, then works with us to ensure that we carry out the action he has ordained.

Rebecca Weaver contends that Augustine's teaching of sovereign grace challenges the "genuinely human character" of prayer, exhortation, and rebuke, by insisting that the interaction between humans and God is actually controlled from outside the human sphere, so that the results of these interactions are based on God's prior decision and not on the interactions themselves.[153] Augustine's belief in unconditional election, the Platonic definition of immutability, and his own theory that evil is the privation of good, all support Weaver's hypothesis and call into question the nature of the relationship between God and humans.

In *Letter 217*, written about the same time as *Grace and Free Choice*, Augustine says, God works on the will to prepare it, in such a way that he "produces a person's will" and moves a person's mind, "so that he gives his assent."[154] The human agent prays, repents, or believes only as God moves his mind to do so. Narve Strand says, "God sees to it that man's will is inwardly prepared, converted, strengthened and sustained unto the end by His unmerited mercy and grace."[155] This unilateral divine action that

---

151. Augustine, *Grace and Free Choice*, 16.32.
152. Ibid., 17.34.
153. Weaver, *Grace*, 2.
154. Augustine, *Letter 217*, 2.5.
155. Strand, "Augustine," 298.

secures the assent of the will undercuts Augustine's early claim that God wants men to serve him freely and not from necessity, since the will has no power to say "No" to this divine action.

Near the end of *Letter 217*, Augustine returns to Prov 8:35, "The will is prepared by the Lord," and reasserts that God does not wait for human beings to believe in him, but converts their wicked wills "with his omnipotent ease, making them willing instead of unwilling."[156] "But we are now speaking about the very beginnings," he writes, "when people who were turned away from and set against God are turned back to him and begin to will what they did not will and to have the faith that they did not have."[157] In closing, he resolves, "you ought undoubtedly to admit that the wills of human beings are anticipated by the grace of God and that God . . . brings it about that human beings will the good that they did not will."[158] When God gives "fully efficacious strength to the will," he produces the will he wants and brings it about that humans will what they did not will. The human will is converted from "unwilling" to "willing" without ever being given the choice to say "Yes" or "No."

Paul Lehman observes correctly, "grace co-operates with us," only in the sense that it cooperates with the good will that God has already produced in us.[159] "He who prepares the will," says Augustine, "begins by working in us that we will and works along with our will in making them perfect."[160] There is no human cooperation prior to this gratuitous work. Weaver concludes, "within the Augustinian scheme, the determination of one's destiny is passing from the human self to divine intervention and the operation of grace is overriding the reality of human agency."[161]

Even as Augustine teaches the operative nature of grace, he continually denies that God "compels the will." He says the will is prepared, directed, produced, and made to act by God, but denies this is compulsion. Rist says, Augustine's analysis of compulsion, "only recognizes external compulsion as compulsion. What we should call psychological compulsions

---

156. Augustine, *Letter 217*, 6.24.
157. Ibid., 7.29.
158. Ibid., 7.30.
159. Lehman, *The Anti-Pelagian Writings*, 224.
160. Augustine, *Grace and Free Choice*, 17.33.
161. Weaver, *Grace*, 18–19.

are not compulsions for Augustine."[162] O'Daly claims Augustine rejects only external compulsion, but does not reject the external causation of the will.[163] The early Augustine argued against either of these possibilities, stating, "Everyone who does something unwillingly is forced."[164] Whether we call it external compulsion or external causation, Augustine believes all human wills are unwilling at the moment they are converted. O'Daly rejects Augustine's denial of compulsion and concludes, "The will is not self-determining."[165]

In Augustine's later works, God's sovereign control of the will includes both believers and unbelievers. He writes, "not only the good wills of human beings which God himself produces out of evil ones and which, once made good by him, he directs toward good acts and toward eternal life, but also those wills which preserve the creature of the world are in the power of God so that he makes them turn where he will and when he wills."[166]

John Rotelle suggests the phrase, "those wills which preserve the creature of the world," is similar to the idea found in *Answer to Julian*, when Augustine said God uses the "vessels of anger" to "adorn the order of the present world."[167] Both are ways to refer to the reprobate. That this is Augustine's meaning is substantiated by the illustrations that follow. He points to the man who cursed David in 2 Sam 16:12, instructing, "Scripture said, 'The Lord told him to,' because by his just and hidden judgment God inclined toward this sin that man's will which was evil because of its own sinfulness." He continues, "God does what he wills even in the hearts of evil persons."[168] He adds, "See, when God wanted to punish the sin of idolatry, he produced it in the heart of the man, with whom he was of course, justly angry."[169] Finally, he writes, "God works in the hearts of human beings to incline their wills to whatever he wills, whether to good actions in accord with his mercy or to evil ones in accord with their

---

162. Rist, "Augustine," 422.
163. O'Daly, "Augustine," 404.
164. Augustine, *Two Souls*, 10.14.
165. O'Daly, "Augustine," 404.
166. Augustine, *Grace and Free Choice*, 20.41.
167. Ibid., 20.41 (see footnote 22).
168. Ibid., 21.42.
169. Ibid.

merits."[170] Augustine uses the same terminology for God's activity in the evil will, which he has used to describe his activity in the good will. Studer objects to this notion of sovereignty, which "shows itself to be an irresistible power. It virtually creates the action of he human will ... The human will is entirely in God's power."[171] This rationale seems to contradict one of the foundational early teachings, which stipulated that God is not the author of the evil a man does.

To conclude *Grace and Free Choice*, Augustine says, "let them imagine what they will about adults," but the Pelagians are stopped by the condition of infants, "who have no will for receiving grace."[172] Once again, we see the influence infant baptism had on his doctrinal development. This ritual demands a grace that is completely gratuitous. In *Grace and Free Choice*, he has defended a role for the will after conversion. God produces faith and assent in the wills of the elect at conversion but then helps them accomplish good works after conversion. He also works in the wills of the reprobate, directing their wills toward evil works that accomplish his purposes. In neither case is there any freedom to say "No" to this efficacious directing of the will.

Rebuke and Grace was written to the same monks, to answer their concerns that his doctrines of grace and election would encourage spiritual laziness and even fatalism. Augustine begins the letter by proclaiming that without grace, human beings "do nothing good whether in thinking, in willing and loving, or in acting. Grace not merely teaches them so that they know what they should do, but also grants that they do with love what they know."[173] The grace at work in conversion is "more powerful" than the grace Adam received in paradise. "For the first grace brought it about that the man had righteousness if he willed to; the second, therefore, is more powerful, for it makes one even to will and to will so strongly and to love with such ardor that by the will of the spirit one conquers the pleasure of the flesh which has contrary desires."[174]

Augustine insists God gave Adam a good will and "a help without which he could not remain in that will even if he willed to, but he left it up

---

170. Ibid., 21.43.
171. Studer, *Grace of Christ*, 133.
172. Augustine, *Grace and Free Choice*, 22.44.
173. Augustine, *Rebuke and Grace*, 2.3.
174. Ibid., 11.31.

to his free choice to will it."¹⁷⁵ He adds, "if either angel or the man lacked this help when they were first created, they certainly would not have fallen through their own fault, because their nature was not created such that it could remain without God's help, even if it willed to."¹⁷⁶ This raises two questions. First, if God can effectually move the will to good without impinging on man's free will, why did he not give this "more powerful" grace to Adam? Second, if Adam would not have been responsible for his fall if he had not been given sufficient grace, why are his descendants responsible when no grace is given to them? Augustine does not give an answer to the first question, but does answer the second, "But now for those who lack such a help its lack is the punishment of sin."¹⁷⁷

Rebuke and Grace places fallen men into three categories. The first group is those who are punished for Adam's sin and are denied any help of grace. The second group consists of those, like Adam, who receive grace but still turn away from God. The third group includes all who receive a better grace than Adam, so they cannot fall, but persevere to the end.¹⁷⁸ We will look at each of these categories to better understand Augustine's doctrines of grace, election, and human willing.

Only those in the latter group are "the elect," who are helped by God's grace, "so that by his gift they invincibly willed what is good and invincibly refused to abandon it."¹⁷⁹ These are the predestined of God, "whose number is so certain that no one is added to them or taken from them."¹⁸⁰ Augustine describes the grace they receive with the adverbs *indeclinabiliter* and *insuperabiliter*. Rist translates these Latin words, "unswerving" and "all-conquering"¹⁸¹ and instructs that this grace "moulds the human will to its own purposes, without any vestige of self-determination remaining for man."¹⁸² Augustine claims God "produces in them" the will to persevere and "they will to (persevere) so strongly because God makes them to will."¹⁸³ He declares, "One should, therefore, have no doubt that human

---

175. Ibid., 11.32.
176. Ibid.
177. Ibid.
178. Ibid., 13.42.
179. Ibid., 12.38.
180. Ibid., 13.39.
181. Rist, "Augustine," 436.
182. Ibid., 435.
183. Augustine, *Rebuke and Grace*, 12.38.

wills cannot resist the will of God . . . Human wills cannot resist his will so that he does not do what he wills, since he does what he wills and when he wills even with the very wills of human beings."[184] "He worked within; he held their hearts, moved their hearts, and drew them by their wills which he himself produced in them."[185] Finally, he asserts, "he has in his control the wills of human beings more than they have in their power their own wills."[186] In the strongest language possible he has stated that God is the cause of human willing. "Unswerving" and "all-conquering" grace causes the will of the elect to "invincibly will" to believe and "invincibly refuse" to abandon faith. No one is able to resist or say "No" to his will.[187]

No one can know if they are among the elect, since "some of the children of perdition, though they have not received the gift of persevering in up to the end, begin to live in the faith . . . and live for some time lives of faith and righteousness, but afterwards fall away."[188] This is the second group—those who receive grace, like Adam, and remain in grace for a while. Since they are not elect, they all inevitably fall away from grace. Henry Knapp says they are "believers," even though they are not "elect." Their faith is not false, since it is a result of grace.[189] It is only temporary faith. Augustine says the will naturally succumbs to temptation and inevitably falls unless it receives the will to persevere.[190] These temporary believers "receive the grace of God, but have it only for a time and do not persevere; they abandon it and are abandoned. For they have been left to their free choice because they have not received the gift of perseverance by the just, but hidden judgment of God."[191] His explanation, "they abandon it and are abandoned" is a bit misleading. He certainly does not mean grace was taken from them because they chose to abandon it. This would imply grace was merited. In truth, he believes that God's decision to abandon them was not based on anything they did or did not do, but was based solely on his good pleasure. That is why he says this abandonment

---

184. Ibid., 14.45.
185. Ibid.
186. Ibid.
187. Ibid.
188. Ibid., 13.40.
189. Knapp, "Augustine," 78–80.
190. Augustine, *Rebuke and Grace*, 12.38.
191. Ibid., 13.42.

reflects God's "just, but hidden judgment." These temporary believers are abandoned by God, then when grace is withdrawn they abandon God.

Surprisingly, Augustine claims they would have received the gift of perseverance if they had willed.[192] Of course, they could not have willed unless God produced that will within them. Strand notes that all who face God's eternal judgment, "either do not receive grace at all, or they receive it only for a season."[193] Persons in the second group are like Adam, who was not given grace "which made him persevere."[194] They receive the grace of conversion and the gift of faith, but they do not receive the grace to persevere. God's choice to withhold this grace guarantees the eventual fall of all who are in the second group.

The first group is made up of those who are condemned for Adam's sin and never given saving grace or the gift of faith. They are "enslaved to sin" from birth and have only freedom from righteousness.[195] As a punishment for Adam's sin, "the assistance necessary to choose and do the good and the freedom to choose between good and evil, which was its fruit, were both lost."[196] Having lost the freedom to choose between good and evil, they retain only "the freedom of spontaneity."[197] They freely and spontaneously choose to do whatever their carnal desires move them to do. They are not free, however, to say "No" to these desires. God's grace alone can provide them the assistance necessary to choose good and this grace has been withheld from them.

Because of his growing conviction that God wills only the salvation of the elect, Augustine attempts another interpretation of 1 Tim 2:4, proposing that "all" means "all the predestined."[198] He urges, "God, then, commands us who do not know who are going to be saved to will that all to whom we preach this peace be saved, and he produces in us this will, pouring out his love in our hearts through the Holy Spirit who has been given to us. Hence, the words, *God wills all human beings to be saved*."[199]

---

192. Ibid., 7.11.
193. Strand, "Augustine," 298.
194. Augustine, *Rebuke and Grace*, 12.34.
195. Ibid., 13.42.
196. Burns, *Development*, 164.
197. Strand, "Augustine," 300.
198. Augustine, *Rebuke and Grace*, 14.44.
199. Ibid., 15.47.

Rist criticizes this interpretation as, Augustine's "most pathetic passage on this subject," because he suggests that God makes us wish all men to be saved, though he does not wish it himself, which would make us "more merciful than God himself."[200] Portalié advises that this apparent contradiction is clarified if we understand that Augustine preached the doctrine of the two wills of God. God's conditional will, that all men be saved is resisted by human freedom of choice, while his efficacious will that only the elect be saved is actually realized.[201] This explanation ignores the fact that Augustine's view of election commits him to the principle that God did not will the salvation of all men from eternity. Since God's will is always undefeated, only his efficacious will truly expresses what he wants. Any "conditional will" is merely a pretense, since everything God wants to happen actually comes to pass. Portalié's theory of two wills of God does nothing to clarify this interpretation of 1 Tim 2:4.

Predestination of the Saints and The Gift of Perseverance

Predestination of the Saints is Augustine's most complete defense of his mature doctrines of election and predestination. Wetzel says, "Without the doctrine of predestination, there is no Augustinian doctrine of grace."[202] It was written around 427 in response to a letter from Prosper of Aquitaine, informing him that many monks in Marseille disagreed with his teaching on predestination. Djuth says their reading of his later works, "led them to conclude that the predestination elements in Augustine's thought signaled a failure on his part to divest himself of the fatalistic view of human action he once espoused as a Manichean."[203] J. N. D. Kelly remarks, "From South Gaul complaints poured in from men who were otherwise his admirers . . . to the effect that his doctrine of predestination paralysed moral effort and verged on fatalism."[204] These monks had probably read the writings of John Cassian, who taught that predestination must be based on what God foresees, since God wills all to be saved. They suggested Augustine's doctrines of predestination and

---

200. Rist, "Augustine," 438.
201. Portalié, *Guide*, 229.
202. Wetzel, "Predestination," 125.
203. Djuth, "Hermeneutics," 281.
204. Kelly, *Doctrines*, 370.

grace destroyed freedom of the will and meant that God himself chooses who will go to heaven and who will go to hell. They feared the reprobate could rightly blame God for negligence and cruelty, doubting how God could be just while making such an arbitrary choice and insisting this view denied God's merciful nature.[205] They sided with the early Augustine and "dismissed the aging Bishop as hopelessly entangled in contradiction and inconsistency."[206]

Augustine begins by denying the first steps of faith come from humans. He says, "if our beginning to believe is not due to the grace of God," then, "the grace of God is given in accord with our merit."[207] He again interprets 2 Cor 3:5 to say we are not sufficient to have "a single thought" as if from ourselves.[208] Modern translations suggest the weight he gives to "a single thought" is not found in the context,[209] but he concludes that this verse proves our will to believe must come from God. He admits to having originally "thought it was our very own and something we had from ourselves that we assented to the gospel which was preached to us,"[210] but he no longer believes this. He has come to believe God causes the will's assent when he gives the gift of faith. He rebukes the brothers, who "have not taken care to progress with me," or otherwise, "they would have found that this question was resolved in accord with the truth of the divine scriptures in the first book of the two which I wrote . . . for Simplician."[211]

He acknowledges that the key change in his doctrinal positions began when he wrote his letter to Simplician. Referring back to this letter, he writes, "In resolving this question I worked hard in defense of the free choice of the human will, but the grace of God conquered."[212] It is noteworthy that he uses the word "conquered" to reflect his mature view of grace's relationship to free choice. Free choice is now conquered by sin, unless grace is given. When grace is given, it "is not rejected by any hard heart. It is, in fact, given precisely in order that the hardness of the

---

205. O'Donnell, *Time and Lives*, 8.
206. Djuth, "Hermeneutics," 282.
207. Augustine, *Predestination*, 2.3.
208. Augustine, *Predestination*, 2.5.
209. C. K. Barrett, *Second Corinthians*, 111.
210. Augustine, *Predestination*, 3.7.
211. Ibid., 4.8.
212. Ibid.

heart may first of all be removed."²¹³ The will's free choice appears to be conquered both before and after grace.

The monks in Gaul objected, "The apostle [Paul] distinguishes faith from works. He says that grace does not come from works, but he does not say that it does not come from faith."²¹⁴ Augustine cites John 6:28-29, "What shall we do in order to do the work of God? Jesus replied and said to them, 'This is the work of God, that you believe in him whom he sent.'"²¹⁵ The implication is that faith is a work, which would merit grace if it were the basis of election. This is similar to the argument in *Deeds of Pelagius*, when he interprets Gal 5:6, "faith works through love," as proof that faith is a work.²¹⁶ His belief that "merit is in the will" makes it impossible for him to accept faith as anything but a meritorious work.

The monks ask, "Why God does not show mercy and give faith to all?" Augustine exhorts them to pray for these unbelievers because God can "make persons willing from unwilling."²¹⁷ "Predestination is the preparation for grace," he says, "while grace is its actual bestowal."²¹⁸ He continues, "when God wills the accomplishment of something which only willing human beings can do, their hearts are inclined to will this, that is, he inclines their hearts who produces in us in a marvelous and ineffable way the willing as well."²¹⁹ Grace is the means by which God produces in human hearts the will to do all that he has ordained from eternity by his predestination.

In *Gift of Perseverance*, Augustine seeks to explain why some who are given the gift of faith do not persevere in their faith. He says, perseverance is a gift of God,²²⁰ which "is not given in accord with the merits of those who receive it."²²¹ Yet, he also says, "This gift of God, then, can be merited by prayer."²²² TeSelle claims Augustine has begun to propose two "divergent theories of predestination," which he labels "predestination to grace"

---

213. Ibid., 8.13.
214. Ibid., 7.12.
215. Ibid.
216. Augustine, *Deeds of Pelagius*, 15.34.
217. Augustine, *Predestination*, 8.15.
218. Ibid., 10.19.
219. Ibid., 20.42.
220. Augustine, *Perseverance*, 1.1.
221. Ibid., 12.28.
222. Ibid., 6.10.

and "predestination to glory."²²³ The first happens prior to any act of human will and causes the will to believe, while the second is conditioned upon human faithfulness. He admits the second view conflicts with Augustine's "explicit statements that predestination has reference only to those who will persevere,"²²⁴ since it is only those who persevere who are the elect. If their perseverance depended on human willing, then election would be conditional. TeSelle believes he may have been moving toward a different understanding of predestination than he had previously taught, which would have allowed a place for "the contingent decisions of free agents."²²⁵ He notes how often Augustine states, "the gift of perseverance is a grace that 'cooperates' with men, and their receiving this gift so that they do persevere, or their falling away is decided not by God, but by themselves."²²⁶ Yet, these statements seem inconsistent with his affirmation that God "produces in us . . . the willing."²²⁷

It would appear Augustine is suggesting those who receive the gift of perseverance, were chosen on the basis of God's foreknowledge of the full course of their lives. TeSelle calls this "predestination after the foreknowledge of merit," but says this "only includes those merits that follow the giving of grace and consist in a steady dependence upon divine aid."²²⁸ He believes Augustine was attempting to develop an alternative doctrine that would have helped him overcome the problems he was discovering in his present position.²²⁹

While Augustine presents divergent notions of the gift of perseverance, he remains committed to the doctrine of predestination. He claims Cyprian taught predestination and insists it has always been part of both the church's teachings and his own teaching.²³⁰ He continues to affirm that all good human willing and action is dependent on the antecedent grace of God.²³¹ After the fall, our heart and our thoughts are no longer in

---

223. TeSelle, *Augustine the Theologian*, 324–5.
224. Ibid., 326.
225. Ibid.
226. Ibid., 328.
227. Augustine, *Predestination*, 20.42.
228. TeSelle, *Augustine the Theologian*, 329.
229. Ibid., 332.
230. Augustine, *Perseverance*, 1.49—20.52.
231. Ibid., 7.13-14.

our power,[232] to such a degree that even baptized believers cannot avoid falling away if grace is withdrawn from them.[233] The church prays for the lost and prays for the gift of perseverance for believers, so that she may be reminded that these benefits come from God.[234] These prayers, however, do not in any way influence or alter what God has predestined. Once again, he points to the case of infants, concluding that God's election is not dependent on human willing,[235] but rests solely on his "inscrutable" choice.[236]

Unfinished Work in Answer to Julian

Augustine's final work is an enormously polemical work. We find Julian defending Augustine's early definition of sin as, "the will to do or to keep that which justice forbids and from which we are free to hold back." Augustine now rejects this definition, stating, "There I defined that sin which is only sin, not that sin which is also the punishment of sin."[237] This "sin which is the punishment of sin," refers to our guilt for the sins of Adam and Eve. "They are the sins of others, but they are the sins of our parents, and for this reason they are ours by the law of propagation and growth."[238] He admits there is "no choice of our own will" in these sins, "and yet they are, nonetheless, also found to be our sins because of the infection contracted from our origin."[239] What he means by "the law of propagation and growth" and "the infection contracted from our origin" appears very close to Traducianism.

Julian asserts freedom of choice means being "immune from compelling necessity; it has in its own power which path it will follow."[240] Augustine rejects this principle and counters that men's choices merely

---

232. Ibid., 8.19.
233. Ibid., 15.38.
234. Ibid., 7.15.
235. Ibid., 11.25.
236. Ibid., 8.18.
237. Augustine, *Answer to the Pelagians III: Unfinished Work in Answer to Julian*, 1.44.
238. Ibid., 1.48.5.
239. Ibid., 1.57.2.
240. Ibid., 1.82.

reflect the will of the omnipotent God.[241] Julian says, Augustine's will, not only lacks freedom to dissent from original sin, but also lacks freedom to dissent from all sins that follow, since he has claimed, "freedom of choice was destroyed by the first sin and remains so crippled thereafter in the whole human race that it cannot do anything but evil."[242] Augustine agrees, but urges that we can still be held accountable for these sins because the will is "moved to sin by many other causes besides the original defect."[243] This may be true, but he has argued in the past that original sin insures that every other cause inevitably moves the will toward evil. Julian denies that fallen man is responsible for necessary sins. In his early works, Augustine would have agreed necessary acts are neither voluntary nor sinful, but now he insists they are culpable.

Augustine attacks Julian, "This is the hidden poison of your heresy: you want the grace of Christ to consist in his example, not in his gift."[244] He valiantly defends the necessity of grace against the Pelagian claim that grace was unnecessary. Yet, the grace he defends is so powerful that it produces willing, so we "undoubtedly believe."[245] Portalié insists the will still has "complete freedom to consent or resist," even in Augustine's later writings.[246] We noted earlier, however, that this freedom does not exist until after the fallen soul has been converted from unwilling to willing. Burns rightly observes that becoming willing from unwilling, "is itself the critical act of faith."[247] Wetzel believes Augustine has handed the human will over to God "root and branch," and judges, "Being subject to another is paradigmatic of a lack of freedom."[248] He objects to the premise that "human consent can be voluntary and necessary at the same time,"[249] a position Augustine himself had defended in his early works.

Julian denies God punishes anyone for sins not "committed by free will," while Augustine insists Adam's sin was sufficient to condemn all human nature. Portalié explains, "we are responsible for the presence of

241. Ibid., 1.93.1.
242. Ibid., 2.105.3.
243. Ibid., 2.146.1.
244. Ibid.
245. Ibid., 2.157.
246. Portalié, *Guide*, 202.
247. Burns, *Development*, 228.
248. Wetzel, "Predestination," 125.
249. Wetzel, *Augustine and the Limits of Virtue*, 202.

this evil within us," by "our participation in the sin of Adam."[250] Augustine proposes that sin "can be in the will, as it was in the will of the first human being; it can also not be in the will, as the original sin of each newborn is not."[251] Bonner rejects this convoluted reasoning, "It is by no means clear how we can be thought of as existing, except potentially in the seed in the body of Adam before Eve conceived by him, and to hold us responsible for our actions, in such a shadowy and inchoative existence, seems to be wholly unreasonable by any standard of ethics."[252]

Augustine's answer to this type of objection is, "when you ask where sin comes from, and you reply, 'from the free will of the one who commits it,' you are thinking only of that sin which is not also the punishment of sin? . . . Human nature, then, sinned in one way when it was free to hold back from sin; it now sins in another way after freedom has been lost when it needs the help of the deliverer. And that former sin was only sin, but this present sin is also the punishment for sin."[253] Even more forcefully, he writes, "It is well known that the first human being did evil by will, not by necessity. But this one who says, 'I do the evil that I do not will' (Rom. 7:19), shows that he does evil by necessity, not by will, and weeping over his wretchedness, he mocks your definitions."[254]

Julian questions God's justice in Augustine's theology, "For this God, who understood in the beginning that an action was not to be counted as sin unless one was free to hold back from it, knew that through all the rest of time all newborns would not be free to hold back."[255] Augustine offers the defense,

> But when this [Adam's sin] happened, the human race was in his loins. Hence, in accord with those previously mentioned natural laws of propagation, which are quite hidden, but very powerful, it followed that those who were in his loins and were destined to enter this world through concupiscence of the flesh were condemned at the same time . . . All the children, then, of Adam were in him infected by the contagion of sin and bound by the condition of

---

250. Portalie, *Guide*, 210.

251. Augustine, *Answer to the Pelagians III: Unfinished Work in Answer to Julian*, 4.91.2.

252. Bonner, *St. Augustine*, 372.

253. Augustine, *Answer to the Pelagians III: Unfinished Work in Answer to Julian*, 5.28.

254. Ibid., 5.50.2.

255. Ibid., 6.22.1.

> death. And for this reason, although they are little ones and do nothing either good or evil by their will, they nonetheless, contract from him the guilt of sin and the punishment of death, because they have been clothed by that one who sinned with the will . . . even though these latter did not commit a sin from which they were free to hold back.[256]

Augustine is once again proposing a very Traducian concept of sin being physically transferred from the bodies of the parents to the bodies of their children. He also removes the power to say "No" from the will in both the will to sin and the will to believe. Humans are condemned for a sin they did not participate in with the exercise of their wills and they are further condemned for sin they cannot hold back from. The only remedy to their situation is a grace which is not offered to all and cannot be resisted by any.

This brings us to the end of Augustine's writings. We have documented dramatic changes in his understandings of grace, election, and the free will. Some believe these changes represent progress, as Augustine's immature philosophical musings evolved into a more biblical theology. Others contend that he compromised his doctrines of free will and grace to accommodate his theory of predestination. In the next chapter, we will evaluate the inconsistencies we have documented in his works. We will give special attention to evaluating how the changes in his doctrines of grace and election have influenced his understanding of the will, sin, moral responsibility, and the character of God.

---

256. Ibid., 6.22.12.

Chapter 4

Evaluation of Augustine's Doctrines of Grace, Election, and the Will

MANY SCHOLARS AGREE THAT Augustine "was chiefly responsible for the triumph of free will against the Manichees and made grace against the Pelagians."[1] Against the Manichees, he defended the voluntary nature of free will. In withstanding the Pelagian error, he led the fight for grace which was more than external teachings and natural capability. He emphasized the need for grace from start to finish in the work of salvation and totally rejected any claims of human merit preceding grace. These were two valuable contributions, among the many that Augustine made to the church's understanding of human nature and salvation.

There is a great deal to like about Augustine's doctrine of grace. If Pelagius had won the debate on grace, the church might well have been bound for centuries by a legalistic, works-oriented version of Christianity. Pelagius's insistence that free choice alone was sufficient for the will to live in obedience to the commandments of God, might have led to an Old Testament version of Christianity. Christian life might have become a continual struggle to strengthen the will to walk in obedience to God's commands, without any help from the Holy Spirit, leading to lives of frustration over the weakness of our wills.

Augustine's insistence on the continual need for grace, not just in the conversion process, but for every moment of the Christian life, delivered the church from this dreary fate and emphasized the completely gratuitous nature of salvation. Christians now believe grace is strong enough to break every bondage of sin and all the habitual chains that have dominated their lives as a result of sin. They have hope that their

---

1. Portalié, *Guide*, 177.

prayers and efforts to evangelize the lost will be answered with a grace that is strong enough to bring light to the darkest heart. New believers are encouraged by the knowledge that grace can give them victory in the struggle with their divided wills. Finally, grace gives confidence to those saints who have persevered in the faith. They know that spiritual growth has been made possible by the presence of grace in their lives, and they are confident grace is strong enough to see them through until the end. For this understanding of the gracious nature of the Christian life we owe a debt of gratitude to Augustine and his doctrine of grace.

Yet, there are also aspects of Augustine's teaching on grace that confound and concern many Christians today, just as they did in his own day. People who appreciate much that he taught are concerned that his later works made original sin so powerful it removed the will's freedom to say "No" to sin, and made grace so powerful it removed will's freedom to say "No" to God's call. In both instances the human will appears to be a powerless victim of deterministic forces.

Wetzel suggests Augustine's view of grace reminds some people of George Orwell's novel, *1984*. He says, the "Big Brother state parodies Augustine's God in all essentials."[2] It possesses omniscience through technology and omnipotence through the strict control of thought and language exercised by the state. When Big Brother finds a rebellious subject who does not love the state, they are taken to the "Ministry of Love" and a conversion process begins. Since Orwell's Big Brother uses external compulsions, like torture, to reorient a person's will and make them love Big Brother, and Augustine disallowed external compulsion of the will, it may be unfair to compare his notion of grace to *1984*. But suppose Big Brother refused to use torture and instead planted a computer chip in the minds of unloving subjects or used brain-washing techniques to control their wills. Wouldn't this still be compulsion? What if Big Brother were capable of performing an operation on citizens while they were unconscious and unaware of the procedure, which would cause them to will whatever Big Brother wanted? Would this be any less depersonalizing than Orwell's Big Brother? Would the citizens be any freer? Yet, Augustine willingly accepted this kind of omnipotent control of human willing. Opponents doubt the sincerity of any love that is produced in the wills of the unloving without their prior consent, even if there is no external compulsion.

2. Wetzel, "Recovery of Free Agency," 123.

Evaluation of Augustine's Doctrines of Grace, Election, and the Will

Some of Augustine's earliest opponents were also concerned that his doctrines of grace and election would produce passive fatalism in Christians. After all, if everything God wills inevitably happens, then human effort appears to have questionable value. Will praying more, fasting more, preaching more, or leaving home to serve as a missionary actually change anyone's eternal destiny? If not, what is the motivation for sacrificing time, money, comfort, and family to do these things? One example of the fatalistic influence of these doctrines may have been evident in the Particular Baptist mission board's reply to William Carey's request to be sent as a missionary to India. They told him, if God wanted to convert the heathen he would do it without Carey's help or theirs. Augustine's critics believe his doctrines of grace and election encourage this type of passive fatalism.

Many who disagree with Augustine's final doctrines of grace and election, do so because these doctrines require him to radically alter his concept of free will. There is certainly debate on this issue. Stump observes, "Even scholars who are careful to make explicit what they mean by 'free will' still don't agree about the nature of Augustine's theory of free will."[3] Peter Brown, among others, judges that there is a severe discontinuity between Augustine's early and later notions of free will.[4] Carol Harrison is among those who argue for continuity.[5] This is an important issue because those who argue for continuity and those who argue against it often have opposing views of what constitutes free will. Does Augustine's early emphasis on free will temper the rigid predestinarian teachings found in his later works, or do the later works represent a significantly altered view of free will? The voluminous quantity of his writings has made our attempt to answer these questions an arduous task, but we have made the journey and are now able to draw some conclusions.

Identifying the Changes in Augustine's View of the Will

The term "will" (*voluntas*) has had a wide variety of meanings in Augustine's works. Djuth suggests the three primary meanings have been: "free movement," "consent," and "love."[6] These three meanings of "will" reveal

---

3. Stump, "Augustine on Free Will," 124.
4. Brown, *Augustine of Hippo*, 140–9.
5. Harrison, *Rethinking*, 198–203.
6. Djuth, "Will," 883.

to us the progressive way that Augustine removes all significant power from the will. In the early works "will" meant free movement to judge the value of influences on the soul and then choose which influences to approve. This free movement required that there be no cause forcing the movement of the will in one direction or another. In the middle works, the will has lost the complete freedom of movement presented in the early works. The penal effects of the fall and the power of grace exert stronger influences on the will, but it maintains the freedom to choose whether it will consent to or dissent from these influences. The will does not choose which influences will present themselves, but it is free to withhold its consent from any it wishes to reject. In the later works "will" is what the soul loves. The will no longer has the power to choose what it will love and it is moved necessarily by the influence of either lust or love. It has also lost the power to choose whether it will consent to or dissent from these influences. Original sin causes it to love evil, with no freedom to love good. Effectual grace causes it to love good, with no freedom of dissent. The will is only free to love whichever influence is strongest, but it is not free to choose between them. The influences on the will causally determine its consent. According to Augustine, if the will could choose to love good without God causing it to do so, then it would be able to make itself better than God had created it. If it could choose to reject "the good will" or "the love of God," it would be able to resist God's omnipotent will.

In its final form, Augustine's will possesses only power of free action. Like an animal, it can act according to its strongest loves or desires, but it is not free to choose what it will love or desire. It must love what it has been causally determined to love, with no power to say "No." It lacks any of its original free movement. Its movements are causally determined by God's predestination. If God chose to withhold grace from them then they will inevitably be driven by lust toward sin with no power to resist. If God chose to show them mercy, then grace moves them through its "unswerving" and "all-conquering power."[7] Both the reprobate and the elect will whatever God predestines that they must.

There are at least four essential qualities of the will that we observed in Augustine's early works. First, the will is the source of each person's character and action. Its choice to say "Yes" or "No" to various desires is what defines a person's character and decides his actions. Second, the

---

7. Rist, "Augustine," 436.

will is a neutral power, which chooses between moral alternatives. This is why the will is morally responsible for its choices. Augustine's use of the phrase *liberum arbitrium* (free choice), "implied to Roman ears, that the kind of decision in question was the kind which can go either way—the kind where an ability to do otherwise than one actually does is present."[8] Third, the will is voluntary and in our power. Its choices must be free from nature, necessity, or compelling influence of any cause. If it lacks the power to restrain its movements, it is neither a will nor free. Fourth, the will maintains the three characteristics listed above, even in Adam's descendants.

As his doctrines of grace and election evolve, these four essential qualities of the will are all disavowed by Augustine. First, the will is denied the power to choose its own disposition. It is said to be a slave to either *caritas* or *cupiditas*, with no freedom to choose between the two. Second, the will is no longer a neutral power. It has no power of choice between moral alternatives. It always chooses to will evil unless it is caused to will good. Third, the will is no longer voluntary nor in our power. At birth, lust exerts an irresistible influence on the will because of original sin. At conversion, grace invincibly moves the will without any power of dissent.[9] Djuth says, "The will appears to be ineluctably disposed towards evil on account of the fall or irresistibly inclined towards good on account of divine election, but in neither case to be moved towards its appropriate object as a result of unbiased choice."[10] Fourth, Augustine claimed that all three of the characteristics listed above were found in Adam and Eve before the fall. After the fall, however, these qualities of the will were lost. Free will is no longer a part of the human nature, unless the will is freed by grace.

While radical changes in Augustine's understanding of free will appear obvious to many scholars, there are many proponents of continuity who are convinced by Augustine's insistence that the doctrine of human freedom he described in his later works was compatible with that which he presented in *Free Will*. Djuth is unconvinced. She writes, "Only by altering his conception of human freedom is he able to reconcile the exercise

---

8. Chappell, *Aristotle and Augustine*, 145–6.
9. Burns, *Development*, 9.
10. Djuth, "Stoicism," 393.

of free choice of will with the prerogative of divine election."[11] Portalié denies Augustine compromised his commitment to free will, though he admits grace has become "the absolute master of all the determinations of the will."[12] If original sin and grace were mere influences upon the will, we would still be able to maintain some degree of free will. When these influences determine the will, we must deny the existence of free will. Though Augustine called any idea of necessary willing a "monstrous assertion,"[13] and insisted that we are drawn neither to virtue nor to vice by necessity,[14] his later works reverse course and argue for necessary willing—wills that are drawn to virtue and vice by necessity. This is not the free will he defended in his early works.

Augustine attempts to explain how the assent or consent of the will can be both voluntary and necessary at the same time. But when he says God "works in us so that we will," God "produces the will in us," and God works the will "in us without us," he is describing a causal determinism that allows for voluntary or free action but does not allow for voluntary or free will. To quote Evodius again, "I know nothing I could call my own if the will by which I will 'yea' or 'nay' is not my own."[15] Augustine originally believed that our assent to the gospel "was our very own and something we had from ourselves," but in *Predestination of the Saints*, he asserted that he no longer believed this. In his later works, the assent of the will is produced in us by external forces and is no longer "our own." Man's powers of self-determination are ruled out, as Augustine advances a form of moral determinism.[16]

Augustine's compatibilist view of free will suggests being "free" is primarily a matter of doing what one wants to do. But Harry Frankfurt says, "freedom of action" is quite different from the concept of "an agent whose will is free."[17] He notes that animals do what they want, though we do not consider them to have free will. This leads him to conclude, "the freedom to do what one wants to do is not a sufficient condition of

11. Ibid., 96.
12. Portalié, *Guide*, 192.
13. Augustine, *Free Will*, 3.3.7.
14. Augustine, *Nature*, 67.78.
15. Augustine, *Free Will*, 3.1.3.
16. Rees, *Pelagius*, 44.
17. Frankfurt, *Importance*, 20.

Evaluation of Augustine's Doctrines of Grace, Election, and the Will

having free will."[18] Freedom of the will means a person "is free to will what he wants to will, or to have the will he wants."[19] Frankfurt requires that a person's second-order volitions, that is, what he wants, must be free to choose which of his first-order desires he will assent to.[20] "A person's will is free only if he is free to have the will he wants. This means that, with regard to any of his first-order desires, he is free either to make that desire his will or to make some other first-order desire his will instead. Whatever his will, then, the will of the person whose will is free could have been otherwise; he could have done otherwise than to constitute his will as he did."[21] Augustine vigorously argued for this level of free will in his early works but denied the will this power in his later works.

Portalié believes Augustine guarded free will, because "the will never determines itself without a motive."[22] Gilson agrees Augustine's "free choice" was always a choice that was "exercised on the strength of motives."[23] This is undoubtedly true, but the key question is whether the will has freedom to choose between motives or the motives exercise such strength that the will has no freedom of choice? Augustine's later works insist that original sin motivates the will toward lust so strongly that the will lacks any freedom to say "No." He also claims grace motivates the will invincibly, again removing the will's power to say "No." In both cases, the will lacks any freedom to choose against these motives. Remembering Augustine's illustration from *Two Souls*, the will he is proposing in his later works is like the first two examples, who were bound and used for sin without ever choosing to be in that condition.[24] Whether original sin or grace is the motive under consideration, if the will never consents to a motive prior to being controlled by it and never has the power to say "No" to the motive, it will not meet Augustine's standard for being a morally responsible will. Rist states, "To be able to reject God was a part of Adam's [man's nature] from the beginning. If such 'power' were to be taken away ... then the nature of man has been fundamentally changed."[25] To the end

18. Ibid.
19. Ibid.
20. Ibid., 21.
21. Ibid., 24.
22. Portalié, *Guide*, 199.
23. Gilson, *Christian Philosophy*, 157.
24. Augustine, *Two Souls*, 10.12.
25. Rist, *Ancient*, 277–8.

of his life, Augustine recognized the power of dissent as an essential part of Adam's nature, but he came to believe Adam's descendants lacked this power. Portalié's proposal of a will that "determines itself" according to motives gives way to a will that is determined by motives that it is powerless to reject. This will lacks the freedom described by Frankfurt, to have been able to constitute itself other than it did.[26] It is not a free will.

TeSelle proposes three factors that constitute Augustine's concept of willing. First is the "suggestion, which occurs to us either through the senses or through our own free association of ideas." Second is "delight," which "is only a movement of the affections; it does not issue in action." Third is "consent," which "is freely given in the center of the self." "In consent we 'cede to,' give in to, ratify some inclination that has already been aroused. Or perhaps we 'resist' the inclination, do not cede to it, but consent to another inclination."[27] He describes how these factors changed as Augustine's concept of the will evolved, "At first Augustine makes the suggestion the area where grace works by calling a man in a way that is congruous to his condition. Then he makes grace the cause of one's delights. God infuses the believer with delight in good. This new delight draws or leads the will, inviting consent. Finally, he says that grace produces consent too. Man's will is steadily removed from the equation."[28]

TeSelle's commentary is very insightful. Initially, Augustine demanded that the will be free to choose what it would delight in. Later, he concluded the fallen will was only capable of delighting in evil, so grace had to produce a delight in the good within the soul, though it left the will free to say "Yes" or "No" to that desire. Finally, he removes all power of choice and says grace produces the delight in good and causes the consent of the will. The causally determined will is free to say "Yes" to grace but is not free to say "No." Without grace it is free to say "Yes" to sin but it is not free to say "No."

Eleonore Stump claims, Augustine's early view of free will was "modified libertarianism."[29] She says, in his early works, he would certainly have agreed that an act of free will must not be "causally determined by anything outside the agent."[30] Defining a first-order volition as, "the will's

26. Frankfurt, *Importance*, 24.
27. TeSelle, "Exploring," 321.
28. Ibid., 325.
29. Stump, "Free Will," 132.
30. Ibid., 125.

Evaluation of Augustine's Doctrines of Grace, Election, and the Will

directing some faculty or bodily power" and a second-order volition as "a will to will something," she contends that in *Free Will*, "a post-fall human being is not able to bring his first-order volitions under the control of his good second-order desires," but "his good second-order desire is enough to enable him to form the first-order volition to ask God to strengthen his will in good."[31] In other words, a man is able to will to be good, but he needs God's help to actually be good.

Stump uses an illustration to show how understanding the difference between first-order and second-order volitions greatly aids our understanding of the free will debate. She describes a smoker, who wants to quit smoking (second-order volition), but is unable to break her habit (first-order volition). The smoker would still have free will if she chose to use a device that causes her first-order volition to be changed. That is, she has free will if she chooses to use a device that overpowers her habitual addiction. So long as the agent, herself, ultimately determines whether or not she will use the device, free will is maintained. However, if an outside force determines whether or not the device will be implanted and used to determine her will, then "it is hard to see why her will should be thought of as free in any sense."[32]

On the basis of this logic, Stump says Augustine "ought to deny that the will of faith is caused only by divine grace." "Even compatibilists," she contends, "generally hold that an agent is not morally responsible for an act if he is caused to do that act by another person."[33] Yet, Stump admits that as Augustine's views develop, he "becomes increasingly insistent that the will of faith is a gift of God in the sense that God alone causes it."[34] In his middle works, he tried to avoid causal determinism by affirming the will's power to consent to or reject grace, but dropped this idea when he came to believe consent itself was a good act which had to be caused by God.

Stump applies Augustine's mature view of free will to her previous illustration, proposing a smoker who had no second-order desire to quit smoking. She reasons that even if a neurosurgeon took it upon himself, without any permission from the smoker, to implant a device that would

---

31. Ibid., 133.
32. Ibid., 136.
33. Ibid.
34. Ibid., 137.

cause her to have the second-order desire to quit smoking, the mature Augustine would have judged that this was a "free choice"[35] when the smoker quit smoking of her own will, even if that will did not originate within her. Stump concludes, "I don't see how he can be saved from the imputation of theological determinism with all its infelicitous consequences."[36]

Though Augustine continues to affirm free choice to the very end, Bonner believes his doctrine of predestination robs it "of any real meaning."[37] Bostock charges him with having gone from a legitimate defense of the will, "to a position where free will was effectively neutered."[38] Both Faustus of Riez and John Cassian rejected his theory of free will because they believed, "human freedom was possible only if the will possessed an innate power to resist both the weight of carnal concupiscence and the divine offer to remove it."[39]

In *Free Will*, Augustine taught that men were different from animals by virtue of the fact they have reason or mind, which is able to rule over their irrational emotions. Bonnie Kent says his argument positing a will depends on two important assumptions: First, "we are justified in holding people, not animals, morally responsible for their actions." Second, "we would not be justified in holding people morally responsible if they did not have a will which somehow transcends natural appetite and natural order of efficient causes."[40] The man with a morally responsible will must be able to judge between desires and appetites of the body and rationally understand which desires are good and which are evil. Then he must have the freedom of choice to decide which desires he will consent to. If he lacks the freedom of dissent, then his will is no more significant than that of an animal.

Augustine radically departed from his early understanding of the will, when he began to view passion, desire, and delight, as "affective modalities of will,"[41] rather than just irrational influences. Fallen man seems to be little different from animals who simply follow their strongest

---

35. Ibid., 136–7.
36. Ibid., 142.
37. Bonner, "They Speak to Us," 295.
38. Bostock, "Origen," 329.
39. Djuth, "Stoicism," 394.
40. Kent, "Augustine's Ethics," 222.
41. Duffy, "Anthropology," 29.

desires. Wetzel contends that being human "requires judgments about what sort of life is appropriate for a human being," and it "requires those judgments to determine an agent's will."[42] In Augustine's later works the will lacks the power to determine itself by deciding what sort of life is appropriate. Instead, it is causally determined by the affective modality of either original sin or effectual grace.

The value God originally placed on free will must have dramatically changed after Adam's sin, according to Augustine's theory of will. At creation, God preferred men to serve him by free will rather than by necessity, but immediately following Adam's sin he is content for the elect to serve him by necessity. Kirwan asks, "If free will was so irrelevant to God that he can cause the elect to do good, why not cause all to do good, or cause Adam to do good from the beginning?"[43] Kelly is also concerned and asks, "If there is no question of the integrity and relevance of the individuality of the soul to be approached by this saving love: if such a consideration does not prevent God's changing his nature and thus securing the acceptance of the will of the creature, then why—should he baulk at performing the transmutative operation in all?"[44]

Why did God consider freedom to choose between good and evil so important for Adam, yet remove this freedom from the rest of human history? Was it only valuable as a way to let sin enter the world? If God is happy to be served by humans who are invincibly motivated by effectual grace, why did he withhold this kind of grace from Adam? God's removal of free will after Adam's sin raises questions about its importance to him. His withholding of efficacious grace from Adam, though it was apparently no impediment to free will, raises questions about whether God wanted sin in the world. His gift of efficacious grace to only some of Adam's race raises questions about his justice, mercy and love. We will explore these issues further in the next section of this chapter.

Affirming God's Just, Loving, and Merciful Nature

Augustine's evolved doctrines of grace and election affect not only his view of man's will, but also his view of God's character and relationship

---

42. Wetzel, "Recovery of Free Agency," 118.
43. Kirwan, *Augustine*, 79.
44. Kelly, *Doctrines*, 367.

to man. When Augustine first proposed his doctrine of unconditional election, he expressed great concern about its implication on the justice of God. He inquires, "How can election be just, indeed how can there be any kind of election, where there is no difference?"[45] He asks, "But how could there be election, or what kind of election could there be, if there was no distinction of merits?"[46] He assures us this choice is not arbitrary, but is based on God's "hidden" justice and perhaps some "hidden merits," for "it is not the case that there is no difference among them."[47] For election to be just and not arbitrary, Augustine recognizes there must be some foundation for God's choice, especially considering how frequently Scripture says God is no respecter of persons. Yet, his concept of "hidden merits" would undo his doctrine of election and his notion of "hidden" justice would make God's justice incomprehensible. His theory of original guilt proclaims God just in condemning all men, though it undermines his early theory of the morally responsible will, since Adam's descendants are condemned for a sin they did not participate in with their own wills. God's justice and man's moral responsibility both fall short of the standards he set for them in *Free Will*. A human judge who condemns all men for one man's crime, then randomly applies the penalties for that crime to some, while pardoning others for no reason but his own good pleasure, would fail to meet even human standards of justice. God's choice to justly punish some of his creation, while mercifully pardoning others with no consideration of anything in them, cannot be rescued from the charge of being arbitrary and leads to questions about God's standard of justice.[48]

How Augustine's doctrines affect our view of God's love and mercy is an even bigger issue than questions about his justice. "All that prevents a larger number of the lost being saved," says Rist, "is the fact that God who intervened to save some declined to intervene to save others."[49] God becomes like the captain of a ship who comes to the aid of a sinking ship with enough life preservers for everyone drowning in the water, but chooses to only rescue some. Augustine and his proponents suggest that the captain's mercy was on display because he freely saved some. Yet, it

---

45. Augustine, *To Simplician*, 1.2.4.
46. Ibid.
47. Augustine, *Eighty-Three Questions*, 68.4.
48. O'Donnell, *Times and Lives*, 8.
49. Rist, *Augustine*, 276.

Evaluation of Augustine's Doctrines of Grace, Election, and the Will

is clear to Augustine's critics that the captain's character would forever be judged by his refusal to show mercy to so many, when it was in his power to be merciful. If God's withholding mercy from the majority of his creation has nothing to do with them, their will, or their choices, but only his own good pleasure, then his merciful character will be severely compromised. The reprobation of the majority of humans, "is ultimately derived from God's 'hating' them . . . or 'hardening' them, and this is nothing else than his deciding not to have mercy on them."[50] Augustine, himself, says God rejected, hated, and withheld mercy from Esau, without consideration of anything foreknown in Esau. The same is true for all the reprobate. According to Augustine, God hates them, rejects them, and withholds his grace and mercy from them because it pleases him to do so. Election is not conditioned on anything in man. Augustine wishes to avoid having the human will set absolute limits on God's redemptive power, but his final doctrines undoubtedly place an absolute limit on God's love and mercy.[51] His doctrine of unconditional election "casts a shadow over God's goodness and mercy."[52]

The Bible affirms that love is so much a part of God's nature, that we can rightly say "God is love." Augustine speaks a great deal about God's love, but his mature theology appears deficient in grasping the extent of God's love for his creation. Initially, Augustine taught God loved all his creation and willed for all to be saved, but unconditional election obligated him to reconsider God's love and reinterpret 1 Tim 2:4. He came to believe that God chose to hate the majority of his creation from eternity and only loves and wishes to save "all the predestined." He acknowledges that the number of the lost will be significantly greater than the number of the elect,[53] yet says the number of the justly damned is of no great importance to God.[54] N. P. Williams quotes John Cassian, one of Augustine's contemporaries, "He whose will it is that not one of these little ones perish—how monstrous sacrilege shall it be thought that He does not will all men to be saved, but merely some in place of all?"[55]

---

50. TeSelle, *Augustine the Theologian*, 179.
51. Wetzel, *Augustine and the Limits of Virtue*, 157.
52. Riches, "Readings," 187.
53. Augustine, *City of God*, 21.12.
54. Augustine, *Letter 190*, 3.12.
55. Williams, *Grace*, 51.

Free to Say No?

God's withholding love and mercy from so many who were victims of Adam's crime, not willing participants, is unfathomable considering the parable of the Good Samaritan. Does God simply pass by the billions who are victims of Adam's sin and desperately in need of love and mercy? Does he require the elect to love their neighbors, while choosing to hate many of them himself? Does he require us to be merciful to all, while withholding mercy from the majority of humanity? Any suggestion that God loves and is merciful to the reprobate by giving them life, sunshine, and temporal blessings does not take into account the Bible's picture of life's fleeting nature. Brief momentary pleasure followed by an eternity of suffering and punishment can in no way be considered a loving or merciful gift. Augustine's doctrines allow us to affirm God's love and mercy for the elect, but leave us with no recourse but to deny his love and mercy for the reprobate.

Final Thoughts

At least four fundamental presuppositions have propelled Augustine toward his final synthesis of grace's relationship to free will. The first was his doctrine of unconditional election. His early works stated frequently that a person cannot rightly be judged or condemned for an action he was powerless to resist and unable to hold back from performing. This type of natural or necessary action would be neither voluntary nor culpable. On several occasions he said this truth was so evident it did not require deep learning or fancy philosophy to be understood. It is a basic notion of justice that makes sense to everyone. Unconditional election forced him to explain why God would condemn all his creation for a sin that only Adam committed with his own will. He suggested Adam's descendants might have committed this sin while they were in Adam's loins, but this wrought havoc on his teaching on moral responsibility, so he concludes that Adam's descendants did not actually sin with their own wills. He goes back and forth between these two explanations but neither provide him with an acceptable justification for condemnation. Whether Adam's descendants were condemned for a sin they did not commit or a sin they did somehow commit when they were in Adam's loins, their moral responsibility remains a questionable proposition. Augustine's doctrine of unconditional election required moral responsibility for a sin committed

Evaluation of Augustine's Doctrines of Grace, Election, and the Will

prior to birth and prior to the exercise of the will. Free will is made irrelevant in the initial act of sin for all of Adam's descendants.

The second presupposition was the theory he drew from the writings of Plotinus, which claimed that God is the only source of good in the universe and evil is the privation of good.[56] This theory led him to propose that man cannot do anything to make the universe better than God created it. Anything good that happens in the universe must be directly caused by God. All good emanates from God alone and cannot be caused by the creation, except as secondary causes. In this kind of universe, God's gift of a free will appears to be a questionable good. Jesse Couenhoven explains Augustine's final position implies that Adam and Eve did not cause the fall, rather the fall happened to them. He contends that Augustine does not blame them for the fall, but rather blames them for being fallen.[57] Their free choice alone could never have chosen good. They were dependent on grace and could only be moved to good by God. Augustine insists that Adam had sufficient grace, but he can never explain why a good will which was helped by sufficient grace, could choose evil. Fendt says he ultimately acknowledged that the angelic fall was a result of deficient grace or not enough aid.[58] If a good will can only produce good fruit and God alone produces the good will, the only reasonable explanation for the fall was that God chose to not produce good in Adam and allowed him to fall. Some have suggested this implies God wanted there to be sin in the world. To be logically consistent, one who takes the position that God is the only cause of good in the world, must also accept the consequent position that whenever there is evil—or the privation of good—it must be because God chose to withhold his goodness. This presupposition removes any role for the human will in our own salvation or any other good that happens in the universe, except as secondary causes.

Augustine's view of omnipotence was the third presupposition that moved him toward his final views of grace and free will. He believed the omnipotent God must certainly run the universe in such a way that only those things which he wanted to happen would actually occur. To insure that his will is always done by men, his grace works invincibly and all-powerfully (*indeclinabiliter* and *insuperabiliter*). Carol Harrison

---

56. Coppleston, *Augustine to Scotus*, 85.
57. Couenhoven, "Augustine's Rejection," 279–98.
58. Fendt, "Between," 218.

and others have tried to downplay the powerful influence of this grace, contending that it is not compelling or overwhelming to the will. She suggests it is unfailing because it calls forth a response that corresponds to man's deepest desires, so that he responds freely. She writes, "Grace can therefore be irresistible without being constraining; unfailing but not necessitating."[59] This description of grace is representative of congruent grace that Augustine taught through his middle works. His later works, however, do not envision grace calling forth a response in the fallen will, since the will is unable to respond to God's call until after it has been converted. The call of God does not correspond to man's deepest desires, but transforms those desires. The will responds and believes freely, because God causes it to respond and believe. This unilateral action of God upon the will is both "constraining" and "necessitating" because the will lacks any freedom to dissent from it. Harrison describes man's delight in God as being love for God. She says, "Such love cannot be said to be determined or coerced: to be love, it must be free."[60] This is certainly correct, but Augustine said the love of God poured into our hearts is, "that by which he makes us love him."[61] This love is not our very own, in the sense that it originates in our choice. It is a love that is produced in our hearts. God makes us love him.[62] Any human who used a drug, brain implant, hypnosis, brainwashing, or any other means of manipulation to cause another person to love them, without having their prior consent or leaving them any means of saying "No" to the process, would have a difficult time convincing society this love was not determined, constrained, or necessitating. Can God's standard of love be lower than our human standards? Contrary to Harrison's opinion, the "love" relationship Augustine is describing appears to be both constraining and necessitating.

Any view of God's omnipotence that suggests God's will is always done in whatever happens in the world has difficulties explaining an enormous portion of Scripture, where God seems to be chastising, criticizing, and punishing humanity for not doing what he willed. The Bible would seem to be full of absurdities where God is commanding certain actions that he has secretly forbidden and forbidding other actions that he has

---

59. Harrison, "*Delectatio Victrix*," 300.
60. Ibid., 301.
61. Augustine, *Spirit and the Letter*, 33.56.
62. Augustine, *Grace of Christ*, 1.12.23—13.14.

secretly commanded. In addition, every time God calls out with compassion for people everywhere to repent, he actually feels no compassion for the majority of humanity and extends them no possibility of mercy. His call to repentance and life would appear to be a cruel hoax toward most humans. Even as he calls the reprobate to repent, he is withholding from them the grace they need to be able to repent. Augustine tried to avoid these absurdities by suggesting God has two wills. Yet he also instructs, "The Omnipotent cannot will in vain."[63] Absolute sovereignty means that whatever God wants, and only what he wants, inevitably happens in the world. From the first sin of Adam to the worst sins of human history, each and every sin that has or will occur was eternally predestined by God. Scott claims the doctrine of omnipotence is so fundamental to Augustine, that whenever he was "faced with a problem that seems to threaten the goodness and justice of God, Augustine never gave any consideration whatever to the alternative of limiting the power or control of the imperial deity over every detail of creation."[64] God's omnipotence was the one doctrine that could not be compromised, "regardless of any consequences it may have."[65] One consequence is that he is forced to deny free will in favor of the causally determined will, which does only what the omnipotent will of God has predestined.

The Catholic practice of infant baptism is the fourth presupposition that significantly shaped the development of Augustine's doctrines of grace, election, and will. TeSelle suggests that if Augustine's view of infant baptism were dropped and the biblical meaning of 1 Tim 2:4 were taken seriously, Augustine might have developed an understanding of grace that was "quite different from the present."[66] He says Augustine could have proposed that grace was necessary for conversion and was offered to every man prior to any merits. This grace could evoke a positive inclination in a man's will, such that consent is the only reasonable response. However, this consent would not be inevitable and could be refused. TeSelle writes, "the point of divergence from Augustine would be this: he thought operating grace worked infallibly and irresistibly to produce a human act, so that only the elect can be called in a congru-

---

63. Augustine, *Enchiridion*, 26.100.
64. Scott, *Augustine*, 218.
65. Ibid., 227.
66. TeSelle, *Augustine the Theologian*, 330.

ous way, while later theologians would prefer to say that operating grace, though it infallibly gives the inclination to act . . . can still be resisted or simply unheeded."[67]

For Augustine to have accepted TeSelle's view he would have had to continue affirming the will's power to say "No." We have shown how he clearly affirmed this power throughout his early works and as late as *Spirit and the Letter*. But when he looked at infants, he recognized that he could not teach the saving nature of infant baptism and still insist the will was necessary for either sin or salvation. The infants who came to him were guilty of sin before they ever exercised their wills and they received salvation while they were still kicking, screaming, and resisting.

His theories of unconditional election, absolutely sovereign omnipotence, evil as the privation of good, and the saving nature of infant baptism made it impossible for him to continue to affirm the freedom of the will to say either "Yes" or "No" to sin and grace. He continues to use the language of assent after *Spirit and the Letter*, but this consent is produced in the will either by God's punishment for Adam's sin or by his grace. In either case it is God alone who inclines the will "to whatever he wills,"[68] "does what he wills and when he wills with the very wills of human beings,"[69] and "has in his control the wills of human beings more than they have in their power their own wills."[70] Augustine's later theology can no longer allow the will to have the power to say "No" to original sin or grace.

Some have judged Augustine's evolved theological system to be brilliant, while others have judged it to be unstable. No one denies that it has been immensely influential in the history of the church. A great deal of both Catholic and Protestant theology has been shaped by Augustine's doctrines of grace, election, and the will. His acceptance of unconditional election in *To Simplician* was the turning point that led to the doctrines of irresistible grace and the causally determined will. These doctrines cannot be combined with his early theory of free will to create a coherent system. The attempt to do so created serious inconsistencies in his own writings. One must reject the foundational definitions of "will," "sin," and

67. Ibid.
68. Augustine, *Grace and Free Choice*, 21.43.
69. Augustine, *Rebuke and Grace*, 14.45.
70. Ibid.

Evaluation of Augustine's Doctrines of Grace, Election, and the Will

"voluntary" in Augustine's early works to be able to adopt his mature doctrines. One has to throw out his illustrations of the falling rock, the hinge, the scale, and the four states of bound sinners in order to accept his final description of the causally determined will. If the findings of this book are correct, those who try to harmonize the early and later views are not being faithful to the clear principles that he establishes in each. The final delineation between these views seems to be his removal of the will's freedom to say "No" to original sin and grace. To rephrase Evodius's insightful comment from *Free Will*, "What possible value is there in having a will that has no freedom to define its own character by choosing the desires and loves it will say "Yes" or "No" to?[71] In what sense would this will be "my own" if it is born guilty of a sin that is not mine and is enslaved to sin that I never freely chose?[72] In what way is faith or love meaningful if they do not originate in my own will and are not my very own?[73] According to Augustine's early works, the will that lacks these essential characteristics is not free. In fact, it is not even a will.[74]

---

71. Augustine, *Free Will*, 3.1.3.

72. Augustine, *Answer to the Pelagians III: Unfinished Work in Answer to Julian*, 1.57.2.

73. Augustine, *Grace and Free Choice*, 7.17; *Deeds of Pelagius*, 15.34; *Predestination of the Saints*, 3.7; *Grace of Christ*, 1.12.23—13.14.

74. Augustine, *Two Souls*, 11.15.

Bibliography

Primary Sources

Augustine. *Answer to Felix.* In *WSA* 1/19: 271–318.
———. *Answer to Julian.* In *WSA* 1/24: 223–536.
———. *Answer to the Pelagians III: Unfinished Work in Answer to Julian.* In *WSA* 1/25: 1–772.
———. *Answer to the Two Letters of the Pelagians.* In *WSA* 1/24: 98–219.
———. *Augustine on Romans: Propositions from the Epistle to the Romans and Unfinished Commentary on the Epistle to the Romans.* Translated by Paula Fredriksen Landes. Chico, CA: Scholars Press, 1982.
———. *Catholic and Manichean Ways of Life.* The Fathers Of The Church: A New Translation (Patristic Series) 56. Translated by Donald A. Gallagher. Washington, D.C.: Catholic University of America Press, 1966.
———. *Christian Doctrine.* In Nicene and Post-Nicene Fathers, ser. 2, 2:515–98. Peabody, MA: Hendrickson, 2004.
———. *City of God.* A Select Library of Nicene and Post-Nicene Fathers, vol 2. Edited by Phillip Schaff. Translated by Marcus Dods. Grand Rapids: Eerdmans, 1956.
———. *Confessions and Enchiridion.* Edited and translated by Albert C. Outler. Library of Christian Classics 7. Louisville: Westminster John Knox, 1955.
———. *Continence.* In *WSA* 1/9: 192–216.
———. *Debate with Fortunatus.* In *WSA* 1/19: 145–64.
———. *Deeds of Pelagius.* In *WSA* 1/25: 336–83.
———. *Eighty-Three Different Questions.* Translated by David L. Mosher. The Fathers of the Church 70. Washington, D.C.: Catholic University of America Press, 1982.
———. *Faith and Works.* In *WSA* 1/8: 221–64.
———. *Free Will.* In *Earlier Writings*, translated by John H. S. Burleigh. Library of Christian Classics 6:102–217. Louisville: Westminster, 1953.
———. *Genesis: A Refutation of the Manichees.* In *WSA* 1/13:39–104.
———. *Gift of Perseverance* In *WSA* 1/26: 191–236.
———. *Grace and Free Choice.* In *WSA* 1/26: 71–107.
———. *Grace of Christ and Original Sin.* In *WSA* 1/25: 403–65.
———. *Letter 143.* In *Letters, Volume 3 (131-164).* Translated by Wilfrid Parsons. Fathers of the Church 20:131–64. Washington, D.C.: Catholic University of America Press, 1955.

Bibliography

———. *Letter 166*. In *Letters, Volume 4 (165-203)*. Translated by Wilfrid Parsons. Fathers of the Church 30:6-31. Washington, D.C.: Catholic University of America Press, 1955.
———. *Letter 190*. In *WSA* 2/3: 263-75.
———. *Letter 194*. In *WSA* 2/3: 287-308.
———. *Letter 217*. In *WSA* 2/4: 51-66.
———. *Letter 98*. In *WSA* 2/1: 426-32.
———. *Literal Meaning of Genesis*. In *WSA* 1/13: 168-506.
———. *Magnitude of the Soul*. Translated by Ludwig Schopp. In Fathers of the Church 4:51-152. Washington, D.C.: Catholic University of America Press, 1947.
———. *On Music*. Translated by Ludwig Schopp. In Fathers of the Church 4:153-379. Washington, D.C.: Catholic University of America Press, 1948.
———. *Nature and Grace*. In *WSA* 1/23: 225-78.
———. *Nature of the Good*. In *Earlier Writings*, translated by John H. S. Burleigh. Library of Christian Classics 6:324-48. Louisville: Westminster, 1953.
———. *Nature and Origin of the Soul*. In *WSA* 1/23: 473-562.
———. *Perfection of Human Righteousness*. In *WSA* 1/25: 289-317.
———. *Predestination of the Saints*. In *WSA* 1/26: 149-90.
———. *Propositions from the Epistle to the Romans*. In *Augustine on Romans: Propositions from the Epistle to the Romans and Unfinished Commentary on the Epistle to the Romans*. Translated by Paula Fredriksen Landes. Chico, CA: Scholars Press, 1982.
———. *Punishment and Forgiveness of Sins and the Baptism of Little Ones*. In *WSA* 1/23: 34-139.
———. *Rebuke and Grace*. In *WSA* 1/26: 109-48.
———. *Retractations*. Translated by Mary Inez Bogan. Fathers of the Church 60. Washington, D.C.: Catholic University of America Press, 1968.
———. *Sermons 94A-150*. In *WSA* 3/4: 147-53.
———. *Soliloquies*. Translated by Ludwig Schopp. In Fathers of the Church 5:335-426. New York: CMA, 1948.
———. *Spirit and the Letter*. In *WSA* 1/23: 150-203.
———. *Ten Homilies on the First Epistle General of St. John*. In *Augustine: Later Works*, edited and translated by John Burnaby. Library of Christian Classics 8:259-348. Louisville: Westminster John Knox, 1955.
———. *To Simplician—On Various Questions. Book I*. In *Earlier Writings*, translated by John H. S. Burleigh. Library of Christian Classics 6:370-406. London: SCM, 1953.
———. *Of True Religion*. In *Earlier Writings*, translated by John H. S. Burleigh. Library of Christian Classics 6:218-83. Louisville: Westminster John Knox, 1953.
———. *Trinity*. In *Augustine: Later Works*, edited and translated by John Burnaby. Library of Christian Classics 8:17-181. Louisville: Westminster John Knox, 1955.
———. *Two Souls*. In *WSA* 1/19: 117-36.
———. *Usefulness of Belief*. In *Earlier Writings*, translated by John H. S. Burleigh. Library of Christian Classics 6:284-323. Louisville: Westminster John Knox, 1953.
———. *The Works of Saint Augustine: A Translation for the 21st Century* [*WSA*]. Edited by John E. Rotelle, translated by Edmund Hill. Part 1: 26 vols.; part 2: 4 vols.; part 3: 20 vols. Brooklyn: New City, 1990-2009.

Secondary Sources

Allin, Thomas. *The Augustinian Revolution in Theology: Illustrated by a Comparison With the Teaching of the Antiochene Divines of the Fourth and Fifth Centuries*. London: James Clarke, 1911.

Arendt, Hannah. *Love and Saint Augustine*. Chicago: University of Chicago Press, 1996.

Babcock, William S. "Augustine and the Spirituality of Desire." *Augustinian Studies* 25 (1994): 179–99.

———. "Augustine on Sin and Moral Agency." *Journal of Religious Ethics* 16/1 (1988): 28–55.

———. "Augustine's Interpretation of Romans (A.D. 394–396)." *Augustinian Studies* 10 (1979): 55–74.

———. "The Human and the Angelic Fall: Will and Moral Agency in Augustine's City of God." In *Augustine: From Rhetor to Theologian*, edited by Joanne McWilliam, 133–49. Waterloo, ON: Wilfrid Laurier University Press, 1992.

———. "Sin, Penalty, and the Responsibility of the Soul: A Problem in Augustine's *De Libero Arbitrio III*." In *Studia Patristica* 27, edited by Elizabeth A. Livingstone, 225–30. Peeters: Leuven, 1993.

Baker, Lynn Rudder. "Why Christians Should Not Be Libertarians: An Augustinian Challenge." *Faith and Philosophy* 20/4 (October 2003): 360–78.

Barr, James. "The Pelagian Controversy." *Evangelical Quarterly* 21/4 (October 1949): 253–64.

Barrett, C. K. *The Second Epistle to the Corinthians*. Black's New Testament Commentary. Peabody, MA: Hendrickson, 1973.

Basinger, David, and Randall Basinger, eds. *Predestination and Free Will: Four Views of Divine Sovereignty and Human Freedom*. Downers Grove, IL: InterVarsity, 1986.

Bavinck, Herman. "The Doctrine of God." Online: http://www.the-highway.com/Bavinck_predestination.html.

Blocher, Henri. *Evil and the Cross: An Analytical Look at the Problem of Pain*. Grand Rapids: Kregel, 1994.

———. *Original Sin: Illuminating the Riddle*. Downers Grove, IL: InterVarsity, 1997.

Bonner, Gerald. "Anti-Pelagian Works." In *Augustine Through the Ages: An Encyclopedia*, edited by Allan D. Fitzgerald, 41–47. Grand Rapids: Eerdmans, 1999.

———. "Augustine and Pelagianism." In *Church and Faith in the Patristic Tradition: Augustine, Pelagianism, and Early Christian Northumbria*, edited by Gerald Bonner, 27–47. Collected Studies 521. London: Variorum, 1996.

———. "Augustine, the Bible and the Pelagians." In *Augustine and the Bible*, edited by Pamela Bright, 227–42. Notre Dame: University of Notre Dame Press, 1999.

———. *Church and Faith in the Patristic Tradition: Augustine, Pelagianism and Early Christian Northumbria*. Collected Studies 521. London: Variorum, 1996.

———. "*Dono perseverantiae, De*." In *Augustine Through the Ages: An Encyclopedia*, edited by Allan D. Fitzgerald, 287. Grand Rapids: Eerdmans, 1999.

———. *Freedom and Necessity: St. Augustine's Teaching on Divine Power and Human Freedom*. Washington, D.C.: The Catholic University of America Press, 2007.

———. *God's Decree and Man's Destiny: Studies on the Thought of Augustine of Hippo*. London: Variorum, 1987.

———. *St. Augustine: His Life and Controversies*. London: Canterbury, 2002.

Bibliography

———. "They Speak to Us Across the Centuries 7: Augustine." *Expository Times* 109/10 (July 1998): 293–6.

Bostock, Gerald. "Origen: The Alternative to Augustine?" *The Expository Times* 114/10 (July 2003): 327–32.

Bourke, Vernon J. "Augustine and the Roots of Moral Values." *Augustinian Studies* 6 (1975): 65–74.

Boyd, Gregory A. *Satan and the Problem of Evil: Constructing a Trinitarian Warfare Theodicy.* Downers Grove, IL: InterVarsity, 2001.

Brachtendorf, Johannes. "Augustine's Notion of Freedom: Deterministic, Libertarian, or Compatibilistic?" *Augustinian Studies* 38/1 (2007): 219–31.

Bright, Pamela, ed. and trans. *Augustine and the Bible.* Bible Through the Ages 2. Notre Dame: University of Notre Dame Press, 1999.

Brown, Montague. "Augustine on Freedom and God." *The Saint Anselm Journal* 2/2 (Spring 2005): 50–65.

Brown, Peter. *Augustine of Hippo: A Biography.* Berkeley, CA: University of California Press, 1967.

———. "Pelagius and His Supporters: Aims and Environment." *Journal of Theological Studies* 19/1 (1968): 93–114.

———. *Religion and Society in the Age of Saint Augustine.* London: Faber and Faber, 1972.

Brown, Robert. "The First Evil Will Must Be Incomprehensible: A Critique of Augustine." *Journal of the American Academy of Religion* 46/3 (1978): 315–29.

Burnaby, John. *Amor Dei: A Study of St. Augustine's Teaching on the Love of God as the Motive of Christian Life.* London: Hodder and Stoughton, 1938.

Burnell, Peter. *The Augustinian Person.* Washington D.C.: Catholic University of America Press, 2005.

———. "Concupiscence." In *Augustine Through the Ages: An Encyclopedia*, edited by Allan D. Fitzgerald, 224–7. Grand Rapids: Eerdmans, 1999.

———. "Concupiscence and Moral Freedom in Augustine and before Augustine." *Augustinian Studies* 26/1 (1995): 49–61.

Burns, J. Patout. "Ambrose Preaching to Augustine: The Shaping of Faith." *Collectanea Augustiniana: Augustine—Second Founder of the Faith*, edited by Joseph C. Schnaubelt and Frederick Van Fleteren, 373–85. New York: Peter Lang, 1990.

———. "The Atmosphere of Election: Augustinianism as Common Sense." *Journal of Early Christian Studies* 2/3 (1994): 325–39.

———. "Augustine on the Origin and Progress of Evil." *Journal of Religious Ethics* 16/1 (Spring 1988): 19–27.

———. *The Development of Augustine's Doctrine of Operative Grace.* Paris: Etudes Augustiniennes, 1980.

———. "Grace." In *Augustine Through the Ages: An Encyclopedia*, edited by Allan D. Fitzgerald, 391–8. Grand Rapids: Eerdmans, 1999.

———. "Grace: The Augustinian Foundation." In *Christian Spirituality, Vol. 1: Origins to the Twelfth Century*, edited by Bernard McGinn, John Meyendorf, and Jean Leclerq, 331–449. World Spirituality 16. New York: Crossroad, 1985.

———. "The Interpretation of Romans in the Pelagian Controversy." *Augustinian Studies* 10 (1979): 43–54.

Byers, Sarah. "Augustine on the 'Divided Self': Platonist or Stoic?" *Augustinian Studies* 38/1 (2007): 105–18.

———. "The Meaning of *Voluntas* in Augustine." *Augustinian Studies* 37/2 (2006): 171–89.

Cain, James. "Free Will and the Problem of Evil." *Religious Studies* 40/4 (2004): 437–56.
Carson, Donald H. *Divine Sovereignty and Human Responsibility: Biblical Perspectives in Tension*. Atlanta: John Knox, 1981.
Carter, Ben M. *The Depersonalization of God: A Consideration of Soteriological Difficulties in High Calvinism*. Lanham, MD: University Press of America, 1989.
Cary, Phillip. *Augustine's Invention of the Inner Self: The Legacy of a Christian Platonist*. Oxford: Oxford University Press, 2000.
———. *Inner Grace: Augustine in the Traditions of Plato and Paul*. Oxford: Oxford University Press, 2008.
———. *Outward Signs: The Powerlessness of External Things in Augustine's Thought*. Oxford: Oxford University Press, 2008.
Chadwick, Henry. *Augustine: A Very Short Introduction*. Oxford: Oxford University Press, 2001.
———. *Augustine*. Past Masters. Oxford: Oxford University Press, 1986.
Chadwick, Owen. *John Cassian*. Oxford: Oxford University Press, 1986.
Chappell, T. D. J. *Aristotle and Augustine on Freedom: Two Theories of Freedom, Voluntary Action, and Akrasia*. London: MacMillan, 1995.
Clark, Mary. *Augustine of Hippo: Selected Writings*. London: Continuum, 1994.
———. *Augustine, Philosopher of Freedom*. New York: Desclee, 1958.
Coppleton, Frederick. *Augustine to Scotus*. Vol. 2 of *A History of Philosophy*. London: Search Press, 1950.
Couenhoven, Jesse. "Augustine's Rejection of the Free-Will Defence: An Overview of the Late Augustine's Theodicy." *Religious Studies* 43/3 (September 2007): 279–98.
———. "St. Augustine's Doctrine of Original Sin." *Augustinian Studies* 36/2 (2005): 359–96.
Courcelle, Pierre. *Recherches sur les Confessions de Saint Augustin*. Paris: Boccard, 1950.
Craig, William Lane. "Augustine on Foreknowledge and Free Will." *Augustinian Studies* 15 (1984): 41–63.
———. *The Only Wise God: The Compatibility of Divine Foreknowledge and Human Freedom*. Eugene, OR: Wipf and Stock, 1999.
Cranz, F. Edward. "The Development of Augustine's Ideas on Society Before the Donatist Controversy." *Harvard Theological Review* 47 (1954): 255–316.
Cress, Donald A. "Creation *de Nihilo* and Augustine's Account of Evil in *Contra Secunduam Juliani Responsionem Imperfectum Opus*, Book V." In *Creation*, edited by Joseph C. Schnaubelt and Frederick Van Fleteren, 451–66. Vol. 2 of *Collectanea Augustiniana: Augustine-Second Founder of the Faith*. New York: Peter Lang, 1990.
Creswell, Dennis. *St. Augustine's Dilemma: Grace and Eternal Law in the Major Works of Augustine of Hippo*. New York: Peter Lang, 1997.
DeCelles, David. "Divine Prescience and Human Freedom in Augustine." *Augustinian Studies* 8 (1977): 151–60.
DePoe, John M. "Why Christians Should not be Compatibilists: A Response to Baker." Online: http://www.johndepoe.com/ChristianCompatibilist.pdf.
De Simone, Russell J. "Modern Research on the Sources of Saint Augustine's Doctrine of Original Sin." *Augustinian Studies* 11 (1980): 205–27.
Dihle, Albrecht. *The Theory of Will in Classical Antiquity*. Sather Classical Lectures 48. Berkeley: University of California Press, 1982.
Djuth, Marianne. "Augustine on Necessity." *Augustinian Studies* 31/2 (2000): 195–210.
———. "Faustus of Riez *Initium Bonae Voluntatis*." *Augustinian Studies* 21 (1990): 35–52.

Bibliography

———. "The Hermeneutics of De Libero Arbitrio III: Are There Two Augustines?" In *Studia Patristica* 27 (1993): 281–89.

———. "*Initium Fidei.*" In *Augustine Through the Ages: An Encyclopedia*, edited by Allan D. Fitzgerald, 447–51. Grand Rapids: Eerdmans, 1999.

———. "Stoicism and Augustine's Doctrine of Human Freedom After 396." In *Collectanea Augustiniana: Augustine—Second Founder of the Faith*, edited by Joseph C. Schnaublet and Frederick van Fleteren, 387–401. New York: Peter Lang, 1990.

———. "Will." In *Augustine Through the Ages: An Encyclopedia*, edited by Allan D. Fitzgerald, 881–85. Grand Rapids: Eerdmans, 1999.

Dodaro, Robert, and George Lawless, eds. *Augustine and His Critics: Essays in Honour of Gerald Bonner*. New York: Routledge, 2000.

Drobner, Hubertus R. "Studying Augustine: An Overview of Recent Research." In *Augustine and His Critics: Essays in Honour of Gerald Bonner*, edited by Robert Dodaro and George Lawless, 18–34. London: Routledge, 2000.

Duffy, Stephen J. "Anthropology." In *Augustine Through the Ages: An Encyclopedia*, edited by Allan D. Fitzgerald, 24–31. Grand Rapids: Eerdmans, 1999.

Edwards, Rem B. "The Pagan Dogma of the Absolute Unchangeableness of God." *Religious Studies* 14/3 (1978): 305–13.

Elshtain, Jean Bethke. "Why Augustine? Why Now?" *Theology Today* 55/1 (1998): 5–14.

Evans, G. R. *Augustine on Evil*. Cambridge: Cambridge University Press, 1982.

Evans, Robert. *Pelagius: Inquiries and Reappraisals*. New York: Seabury, 1968.

Feinberg, John. "God Ordains All Things." *Predestination & Free Will: Four Views of Divine Sovereignty & Human Freedom*, edited by David Basinger and Randall Basinger, 17–44. Downers Grove, IL: InterVarsity, 1986.

Fendt, Gene. "Between a Pelagian Rock and a Hard Predestinarianism: The Currents of Controversy in *City of God* 11 and 12." *The Journal of Religion* 81/2 (2001): 211–27.

Fiedrowicz, Michael. Introduction to *The Enchiridion on Faith, Hope and Charity. On Christian Belief*, edited by Boniface Ramsey, 265–72. Hyde Park, NY: New City, 2005.

Fitzgerald, Allan D, ed. *Augustine Through the Ages: An Encyclopedia*. Grand Rapids: Eerdmans, 1999.

Flew, Antony. "Compatibilism, Free Will, and God." *Philosophy* 48/185 (1973): 231–44.

Frankfurt, Harry G. *The Importance of What We Care About: Philosophical Essays*. New York: Cambridge University Press, 1988.

Frend, W. H. C. *The Donatist Church: A Movement of Protest in Roman North Africa*. Oxford: Clarendon, 1952.

Gerrish, Brian. "Sovereign Grace: Is Reformed Theology Obsolete?" *Interpretation* 57/1 (2003): 45–57.

Gilbert, Neal V. "The Concept of Will in Early Latin Philosophy." *Journal of the History of Philosophy* 1/1 (1963): 17–35.

Gilson, Etienne. *Christian Philosophy of Saint Augustine*. London: Victor Gallanz, 1961.

Greer, Rowan A. "Augustine's Transformation of the Free Will Defence." In *Faith and Philosophy* 13/4 (1996): 471–86.

———. "Sinned We All in Adam's Fall?" In *The Social World of the First Christians: Essays in Honor of Wayne A. Meeks*, edited by L. Michael White and O. Larry Yarbrough, 382–94. Minneapolis, MN: Fortress, 1995.

Hamilton, Robert L. "Philosophical Reflections on Free Will." July 13, 2002. Online: http://evangelicalarminians.org/files/Hamilton.%20Philosophical%20Reflections%20on%20Free%20Will.pdf.

Bibliography

Harmless, William. *Augustine and the Catechumenate*. Collegeville, MN: Liturgical Press, 1995.

———. "Christ the Pediatrician: Infant Baptism and Christological Imagery in the Pelagian Controversy." *Augustinian Studies* 28 (1997): 7–34.

Harrison, Carol. *Augustine: Christian Truth and Fractured Humanity*. Oxford: Oxford University Press, 2000.

———. *Beauty and Revelation in the Thought of Saint Augustine*. Oxford: Clarendon, 1992.

———. "*Delectatio Victrix*: Grace and Freedom in Saint Augustine." In *Studia Patristica* 27 (1993): 298–302.

———. *Rethinking Augustine's Early Theology: An Argument for Continuity*. Oxford: Oxford University Press, 2006.

Harrison, Simon. *Augustine's Way Into the Will: The Theological and Philosophical Significance of* De Libero Arbitrio. Oxford: Oxford University Press, 2006.

———. "Do We Have a Will?" In *The Augustinian Tradition*, edited by Gareth B. Matthews, 195–205. Berkeley: University of California Press, 1999.

Hasker, William. "A Philosophical Perspective." In *The Openness of God: A Biblical Challenge to the Traditional Understanding of God*, edited by Clark Pinnock, 126–54. Downers Grove, IL: InterVarsity, 1994.

Hick, John. *Evil and the God of Love*. Glasgow: Collins, 1979.

Holtzen, Thomas L. "The Therapeutic Nature of Grace in St. Augustine's *De Gratia et Libero Arbitrio*." *Augustinian Studies* 31/1 (2000): 93–120.

Kane, Robert. *The Significance of Free Will*. Oxford: Oxford University Press, 1993.

Kaufmann, Peter Iver. "The Lesson of Conversion: A Note on the Question of Continuity in Augustine's Understanding of Grace and Human Will." *Augustinian Studies* 11 (1980): 49–64.

Kelly, J. N. D. *Early Christian Doctrines*. San Francisco: Harper Collins, 1978.

Kent, Bonnie. "Augustine's Ethics." In *The Cambridge Companion to Augustine*, edited by Eleonore Stump and Norman Kretzmann, 205–33. Cambridge: Cambridge University Press, 2001.

Kirwan, Christopher. *Augustine*. London: Routledge, 1989.

Knapp, Henry. "Augustine and Owen on Perseverance." *Westminster Theological Journal* 62/1 (2000): 65–87.

Knuuttila, Simo. "The Emergence of the Logic of Will in Medieval Thought." In *The Augustinian Tradition*, edited by Gareth B. Matthews, 206–21. Berkeley: University of California Press, 1999.

Lamberigts, Mathijs. "Was Augustine a Manichaean? The Assessment of Julian of Aeclanum." In *Augustine and Manichaeism in the Latin West: Proceedings of the Fribourg-Utrecht International Symposium of the International Association of Manichaean Studies (IAMS)*, edited by, Johannes Van Oort, Otto Wermelinger, and Gregor Wurst, 113–36. Leiden: Brill, 2001.

———. "Predestination." In *Augustine Through the Ages: An Encyclopedia*, edited by Allan D. Fitzgerald, 677–79. Grand Rapids: Eerdmans, 1999.

Lancel, Serge. *Saint Augustin*. Paris: Fayard, 1999.

Lane, Anthony N. S. "Did the Apostolic Church Baptise Babies? A Seismological Approach." *Tyndale Bulletin* 55/1 (2004): 109–30.

Lee, Kam-Lun Edwin. *Augustine, Manichaeism and the Good*. Ottawa: Saint Paul University, 1996.

Bibliography

Lehman, Paul. "The Anti-Pelagian Writings." In *A Companion to the Study of St. Augustine*, edited by R. W. Battenhouse. New York: Oxford University Press, 1955.

MacDonald, Scott. "Primal Sin." In *The Augustinian Tradition*, edited by Gareth B. Matthews, 110–39. Berkeley: University of California Press, 1999.

Mandouze, Andre. *Saint Augustin: L'Aventure de Raison et de Grace*. Paris: Etudes Augustiniennes, 1968.

Mann, William E. "Augustine on Evil and Original Sin." In *The Cambridge Companion to Augustine*, edited by Eleonore Stump and Norman Kretzmann, 40–48. Cambridge: Cambridge University Press, 2001.

———. "Inner-Life Ethics." In *The Augustinian Tradition*, edited by Gareth B. Matthews, 140–65. Berkeley: University of California Press, 1999.

Markus, R. A. *Augustine: A Collection of Critical Essays*. Garden City, NJ: Anchor, 1972.

———. *Sacred and Secular: Studies on Augustine and Latin Christianity*. London: Variorum, 1994.

———. *Saeculum: History and Society in the Theology of Saint Augustine*. Cambridge: Cambridge University Press, 1970.

Marrou, Henri. *Saint Augustin et la Fin de la Culture Antique*. Paris: Boccard, 1948.

Marston, Paul and Roger Forster. *God's Strategy in Human History*. Eugene, OR: Wipf and Stock, 2000.

Matthews, Alfred Warren. *The Development of St. Augustine from Neoplatonism to Christianity, 386–391 A. D.* Washington, D. C. : University Press of America, 1980.

Matthews, Gareth B., ed. *The Augustinian Tradition*. Berkeley: University of California Press, 1999.

Mendelson, Michael. "Saint Augustine." *Stanford Encyclopedia of Philosophy*. Online: http://plato.stanford.edu/entries/augustine.

Merdinger, J. E. *Rome and the African Church in the Time of Augustine*. New Haven, CT: Yale University Press, 1997.

Miles, Margaret. *Desire and Delight: A New Reading of Augustine's* Confessions. Eugene, OR: Wipf and Stock, 2006.

Morris, John. "Pelagian Literature." *Journal of Theological Studies* 16 (1965): 26–60.

Most, William. "St. Augustine on Grace and Predestination." Online: http://www.ewtn.com/library/THEOLOGY/AUGUSTIN.htm.

Needham, N. R. *The Triumph of Grace: Augustine's Writings on Salvation*. London: Evangelical Press, 2000.

O'Daly, Gerald. "Augustine." In *From Aristotle to Augustine*, edited by David Furley, 399–408. Vol. 2 of *Routledge History of Philosophy*. London: Routledge, 1999.

———. *Augustine's Philosophy of Mind*. Berkeley: University of California Press, 1987.

O'Connell, Robert. "De Libero Arbitrio I: Stoicism Revisited." *Augustinian Studies* 1 (1970): 49–68.

———. *Images of Conversion in St. Augustine's Confessions*. New York: Fordham University Press, 1996.

O'Donnell, James J. *Augustine: A New Biography*. New York: HarperCollins, 2005.

———. "Augustine: His Time and Lives." In *The Cambridge Companion to Augustine*, edited by Eleonore Stump and Norman Kretzmann, 8–25. Cambridge: Cambridge University Press, 2001.

O'Meara, John J. *The Young Augustine*. New York: Alba House, 2001.

Pagels, Elaine H. *Adam and Eve and the Serpent in Genesis 1–3*. New York: Random House, 1988.

Bibliography

Pelikan, Jaroslav. *The Christian Tradition: A History of the Development of Doctrine*. Chicago: University of Chicago Press, 1971.
Pinnock, Clark H. *Grace Unlimited*. Eugene, OR: Wipf and Stock, 1999.
Piper, John. *The Legacy of Sovereign Joy: God's Triumphant Joy in the Lives of Augustine, Luther, and Calvin*. Wheaton: Crossway, 2000.
Platinga, Alvin. "Augustinian Christian Philosophy." In *The Augustinian Tradition*, edited by Gareth B. Matthews, 1–26. Berkeley: University of California Press, 1999.
———. *God, Freedom and Evil*. Grand Rapids: Eerdmans, 1974.
Plummer, Eric. *Augustine's Commentary on Galatians: Introduction, Text, Translation, and Notes*. Oxford: Oxford University Press, 2003.
Portalié, Eugene. *A Guide to the Thought of Saint Augustine*. Chicago: Regnery, 1960.
Quinn, Philip L. "Disputing the Augustinian Legacy: John Locke and Jonathan Edwards on Romans 5:12–19." In *The Augustinian Tradition*, edited by Gareth B. Matthews, 233–50. Berkeley: University of California Press, 1999.
Rees, B. R. *Pelagius: Reluctant Heretic*. Wolfboro, NH: Boydell, 1988.
Riches, John K. "Readings of Augustine on Paul: Their Impact on Critical Studies of Paul." In *Engaging Augustine on Romans*, edited by Daniel Patte and Eugene TeSelle, 173–98. Harrisburg, PA: Trinity, 2002.
Reichenback, Bruce. *Evil and a Good God*. New York: Fordham University Press, 1982.
Rigby, Paul. "Original Sin." In *Augustine Through the Ages: An Encyclopedia*, edited by Allan D. Fitzgerald, 607–14. Grand Rapids: Eerdmans, 1999.
Rist, John M. *Augustine: Ancient Thought Baptized*. Cambridge: Cambridge University Press, 1994.
———. "Augustine on Free Will and Predestination." *Journal of Theological Studies* 20/2 (October 1969): 420–47.
Rogers, Katherin A. "Augustine's Compatibilism." *Religious Studies* 40/1 (2004): 415–35.
———. "Fall." In *Augustine Through the Ages: An Encyclopedia*, edited by Allan D. Fitzgerald, 351–52. Grand Rapids: Eerdmans, 1999.
Rotelle, John E. "The Background Correspondence." *Grace and Free Choice*. Vol. 1-26 of *WSA*. Hyde Park, NY: New City, 1999.
———. Introduction to *Punishment and Forgiveness of Sins and the Baptism of Little Ones*. Vol. 1-23 of *WSA*. Hyde Park, NY: New City, 1997.
———. Introduction to *The Grace of Christ and Original Sin*. Vol. 1-23 of *WSA*. Hyde Park, NY: New City, 1997.
———. Introduction to *Grace and Free Choice*. Vol. 1-26 of *WSA*. Hyde Park, NY: New City, 1999.
Rupp, E. Gordon and Philip S. Watson. *Luther and Erasmus: Free Will and Salvation*. Philadelphia: Westminster, 1969.
Schaff, Philip. *History of the Christian Church*. Vol. 3 of *NPNF*. Grand Rapids: Eerdmans, 1960.
Schnaubelt, Joseph C., and Frederic Van Fleteren, eds. *Augustine: Second Founder of the Faith*. In *Collectanea Augustiniana*. New York: Peter Lang, 1990.
Scott, T. Kermit. *Augustine: His Thought in Context*. New York: Paulist, 1995.
Sell, Alan P. F. "Augustine Versus Pelagius: A Cautionary Tale of Perennial Importance." *Calvin Theological Journal* 12 (1977): 117–43.
Smith, Thomas A. *De Gratia: Faustus of Riez's Treatise on Grace and Its Place in the History of Theology*. Notre Dame, IN: Notre Dame Press, 1990.

Bibliography

Sontag, F. "Augustine's Metaphysics and Free Will." *Harvard Theological Review* 60 (1967): 297–306.

Springstead, Eric O. "Will and Order: The Moral Self in Augustine's *De Libero Arbitrio*." *Augustinian Studies* 29/2 (1998): 77–96.

Staley, Kevin M. "God's Personal Freedom: A Response to Katherin Rogers." *The Saint Anselm Journal* 1/1 (2003): 9–16.

Stark, Judith. "The Dynamics of the Will in Augustine's Conversion." In *Dynamics*, edited by Joseph C. Schnaubelt and Frederick Van Fleteren, 45–64. Vol. 2 of *Collectanea Augustiniana: Augustine—Second Founder of the Faith*. New York: Peter Lang, 1990.

Strand, Narve. "Augustine on Predestination and Divine Simplicity." In *Studia Patristica* 38, edited by M. F. Wiles and E. J. Yarnold, 290–305. Leuven: Peeters, 2001.

Studer, Basil. *The Grace of Christ and the Grace of God in Augustine of Hippo: Christocentrism or Theocentrism?* Collegeville, MN: Liturgical Press, 1997.

Stump, Eleonore. "Alternative Possibilities and Moral Responsibility: The Flicker of Freedom." *The Journal of Ethics* 3/4 (1999): 299–324.

———. "Augustine on Free Will." In *The Cambridge Companion to Augustine*, edited by Eleonore Stump and Norman Kretzmann, 124–47. Cambridge: Cambridge University Press, 2001.

Sweeney, Leo. "'Was St. Augustine a Neoplatonist or a Christian?' Old Question, New Approach." In *Collectanea Augustiniana: Augustine Second Founder of the Faith*, edited by Joseph C. Schnaublet et al., 403–20. New York: Peter Lang, 1990.

Tennant, F. R. *The Sources of the Doctrines of the Fall and Original Sin*. Cambridge: Cambridge University Press, 1903.

TeSelle, Eugene. *Augustine the Theologian*. London: Burns and Oates, 1970.

———. *Augustine*. Nashville: Abingdon, 2006.

———. "Engaging Scripture: Patristic Interpretation of the Bible." In *Engaging Augustine on Romans*, edited by Daniel Patte and Eugene TeSelle, 1–62. Harrisburg, PA: Trinity, 2002.

———. "Exploring the Inner Conflict: Augustine's Sermons on Romans 7 & 8." In *Augustine: Biblical Exegete*, edited by Frederick Van Fleferen and Joseph C. Schnaubelt, 313–45. New York: Peter Lang, 2001.

———. "Faith." *Augustine Through the Ages: An Encyclopedia*, edited by Allan D. Fitzgerald, 347–50. Grand Rapids: Eerdmans, 1999.

———. "Nature and Grace in Augustine's Expositions of Genesis I, 1–5." *Recherches Augustiniennes* 5 (1968): 95–137.

Teske, Roland. "*Libero Arbitrio, De*." In *Augustine Through the Ages: An Encyclopedia*, edited by Allan D. Fitzgerald, 494–95. Grand Rapids: Eerdmans, 1999.

Tilley, Maureen A. *The Bible in Christian North Africa: The Donatist World*. Minneapolis: Fortress, 1997.

Torrance, Thomas F. *The Doctrine of Grace in the Apostolic Fathers*. Edinburgh: Oliver and Boys, 1948.

Van der Meer, Frederick. *Augustine the Bishop: The Life and Work of a Father of the Church*. London: Sheed and Ward, 1961.

Van Fleteren, Frederick. "St. Augustine's Theory of Conversion." In *Collectanea Augustiniana: Augustine—Second Founder of the Faith*, edited by Joseph C. Schnaublet and Frederic Van Fleteren, 65–80. New York: Peter Lang, 1990.

Van Inwagen, Peter. *An Essay on Free Will*. Oxford: Oxford University Press, 1983.

Bibliography

———. "The Incompatibility of Free Will and Determinism." *Philosophical Studies* 27 (1975): 185–99.
Van Riel, Gerd. "Augustine's Will, an Aristotelian Notion? On the Antecedents of Augustine's Doctrine of the Will." *Augustinian Studies* 38/1 (2007): 255–79.
Weaver, Rebecca Harden. *Divine Grace and Human Agency: A Study of the Semi-Pelagian Controversy*. Macon, GA: Mercer University Press, 1996.
Wetzel, James. *Augustine and the Limits of Virtue*. Cambridge: Cambridge University Press, 1992.
———. "Augustine on Free Will and Predestination." In *Augustine and His Critics*, edited by Robert Dodaro and George Lawless, 124–41. London: Routledge, 2000.
———. "Pelagius Anticipated: Grace and Election in Augustine's *Ad Simplicianum*." In *Augustine: From Rhetor to Theologian*, edited by Joanne McWilliam, 121–32. Waterloo: Laurier University Press, 1992.
———. "Predestination, Pelagianism, and Foreknowledge." In *The Cambridge Companion to Augustine*, edited by Eleonore Stump and Norman Kretzmann, 49–58. Cambridge: Cambridge University Press, 2001.
———. "The Recovery of Free Agency in the Theology of St. Augustine." *Harvard Theological Review* 80/1 (1987): 101–25.
———. "*Simplicianum, Ad.*" In *Augustine Through the Ages: An Encyclopedia*, edited by Allan D. Fitzgerald, 798–99. Grand Rapids: Eerdmans, 1999.
———. "Snares of Truth: Augustine on Free Will and Predestination." In *Augustine and His Critics*, edited by Robert Dodaro and George Lawless, 124–41. New York: Routledge, 2000.
———. "Will and Interiority in Augustine: Travels in an Unlikely Place." *Augustinian Studies* 33/2 (2002): 139–60.
Wiles, Maurice. *The Christian Fathers*. London: SCM, 1966.
Williams, N. P. *The Grace of God*. London: Hodder and Stoughton, 1930.
Willis, Geoffrey Grimshaw. *Saint Augustine and the Donatist Controversy*. Eugene, OR: Wipf and Stock, 1950.
Wills, Garry. *Saint Augustine's Memory*. Middlesex, UK: Penguin, 2002.
Wilson-Kastner, Patricia. "Grace as Participation in the Divine Life in the Theology of Augustine of Hippo." *Augustinian Studies* 7 (1976): 135–52.

www.ingramcontent.com/pod-product-compliance
Lightning Source LLC
Chambersburg PA
CBHW072153160426
43197CB00012B/2366